Geronimo! U.S. Airborne Uniforms, Insignia & Equipment in World War II *Bill Rentz*. Explores the uniforms, insignia, and equipment of American Airborne, Glider, Troop Carrier, and Airborne Engineers in World War II. Detailed images of individual items, multi-side views of full combat rig, and over 100 World War II photos, most unpublished, showing the uniforms and equipment as worn by the troops. Also a comparative section with both British and German airborne gear. An important reference work for the airborne collector, reenactor, historian and veteran.
Size: 9"x12" • over 630 color and b/w photos • 192 pp. • ISBN: 0-7643-0677-4 • hard cover • $59.95

Paramarine! Uniforms and Equipment of Marine Corps Parachute Units in World War II *Chris Mason*. *Paramarine*! is devoted to the Marines and Sailors of the Marine Corps parachute units of World War II. It explores in fascinating detail their unique, specially-designed uniforms, equipment, weapons and insignia. For the first time, over 500 photographs and images from World War II and modern collections have been assembled in one volume and combined with a wealth of facts and information about all aspects of Paramarine gear and training. *Paramarine* is the latest in Schiffer's series of studies on the airborne forces of World War II and is a must for historians and Marine Corps and Airborne collectors around the world.
Size: 9"x12" • over 500 color & b/w photos • 240 pp. • ISBN: 0-7643-1924-8 • hard cover • $69.95

We are always interested in working with authors or collectors on wonderful book ideas. Contact us at **www.schifferbooks.com,** and page down to "For Authors – Submit a Book Proposal." Or call or write to us about your proposal.

Talk with your local bookseller. Their knowledge is one of the best tools in finding the correct book, and we all need to support them.

* Peter Schiffer and Team *
Designed & composed in America.
Printed in China.

SS-Heimwehr Danzig

SS-Heimwehr Danzig

in Poland 1939

Rolf Michaelis

Schiffer Military History
Atglen, PA

Book translation by Christine Wisowaty

Book Design by Ian Robertson.

Copyright © 2008 by Schiffer Publishing.
Library of Congress Control Number: 2007940876

Printed in China.
ISBN: 978-0-7643-2943-2

This book was originally published in German under the title
Die SS-Heimwehr Danzig im Polenfeldzug by Michaelis-Verlag

We are interested in hearing from authors with book ideas on related topics.

Published by Schiffer Publishing Ltd.
4880 Lower Valley Road
Atglen, PA 19310
Phone: (610) 593-1777
FAX: (610) 593-2002
E-mail: Info@schifferbooks.com.
Visit our web site at: www.schifferbooks.com
Please write for a free catalog.
This book may be purchased from the publisher.
Please include $3.95 postage.
Try your bookstore first.

In Europe, Schiffer books are distributed by:
Bushwood Books
6 Marksbury Avenue
Kew Gardens
Surrey TW9 4JF, England
Phone: 44 (0) 20 8392-8585
FAX: 44 (0) 20 8392-9876
E-mail: Info@bushwoodbooks.co.uk.
Visit our website at: www.bushwoodbooks.co.uk
Free postage in the UK. Europe: air mail at cost.
Try your bookstore first.

Contents

Preface

Danzig, which has a centuries-old history, has become synonymous with the outbreak of the Second World War.

Having become a political concern in the course of tensions in Europe at the end of the 30s, the Free City initially would have been without any protection against enemy troops in a war with Poland.

In order to prevent this, the Danzig Senate ordered the formation of local defense units. One of these formations was the *SS-Heimwehr Danzig*.

Due to the existing conflicts with Poland, roughly 500 young citizens of Danzig, who believed their home was threatened, and wished for the propagated annexation to the German Reich, reported to this formation—initially referred to as the "*Einwohner* (resident)" unit.

This book tells of the history of this troop, as well as the political background of its mission. Home and foreign institutions, as well as numerous contemporary witnesses were involved in order to complete this work.

The politics in Europe during the 30s and 40s brought about not only the loss of home for millions of people, but also unspeakable suffering, death, and destruction. May the reader keep this in mind!

Berlin, November 1999
Rolf Michaelis

Foreword
May 23, 1990

"SS-Heimwehr Danzig? Who knew this small troop or knows this small unit, which was conceived as the Schutztruppe (protection force) *for the Free City of Danzig?*

Their formation began in the year 1939, when political tensions between Germany and Poland were on the rise.

After more than 50 years, a young man endeavored to produce a document on the SS-Heimwehr Danzig.

It was a difficult task, because there were no records available in the archives. Why, how, and where was the Heimwehr *formed? Their military mission in Dirschau, and then on the Oxhöfter Kämpe.*

Those of us from the former SS-Heimwehr Danzig *who are still alive ask that the author is not denied recognition."*

Wolfram Schneider
(November 12, 1912-August 22, 1992)
Former Commander of the *Kraftfahrkompanie*

The Formation of the *SS-Heimwehr Danzig*

With the defeat of the First World War, there were numerous changes for Germany. As a result of the Versailles Treaty, the German Reich was permitted to maintain initially 200,000, and ultimately only 100,000 soldiers. Among countless cessions of land and occupations by Allied troops (for example, Silesia or the Rhineland), a wide territorial corridor was laid by the province of West Prussia, which was to secure the newly formed Poland access to the sea. The capital of West Prussia, Danzig,[1] received the status of a Free City in 1920, and was under the control of a commissioner from the League of Nations. While no military could be stationed in Danzig in accordance with the Versailles Treaty, on February 7, 1920, the last German troop, the *Leibhusaren,* left the city. In the event of a potential attack resulting from outer or inner disturbances, protection was to be provided by Poland, according to the decision by the League of Nations on June 22, 1921.

With Hitler's seizure of power on January 30, 1933, there was a turnaround in Danzig. With the election on May 28, 1933, the National Socialists received overall majority, with 50.02% in the Danzig *Volkstag*. Albert Forster[2] was appointed *Gauleiter* by Hitler, and was able to continually strengthen the NSDAP due to the existing tensions with Poland, although he—possibly due to his Franconian mentality—was not a favored Politician.

On January 1934 a German-Polish Nonaggression Pact and Communications Agreement came about. In spring 1935 Göring went a step further and expressed, opposite the Polish *Staatschef* Marschall Pilsudski, the idea of a joint German-Polish front against the Soviet Union.[3]

---

[1]   In the 10th century on the Mottlau, shortly before the mouth into the Vistula, a settlement already existed—later known as Danzig. After the construction of the St. Katharinen-Kirche at the end of the 12th century and the St. Marien-Kirche in 1224, Fürst Swantopolk from Pomerania transformed the settlement into a city of German rule. When the Herzöge from Pomerania died out in 1294, inheritance disputes for Danzig erupted. After there was no agreement reached between Brandenburg, Böhmen, and Herzog Wladislaw Lokietek from Greater Poland, in 1308 the Herzog called for help from the strengthened German order, which obtained the area from Brandenburg in 1309 in the Treaty of Soldin for 10,000 silver marks. A member of the Hanseatic League since 1361, Danzig broke from the declining German order in 1454, and recognized the sovereignty of the Polish king; it remained, however, independent de facto. In 1772 the northwestern section of Poland had fallen to Prussia through the first Polish division, and was from then on named West Prussia. In the course of the second division of Poland in 1793 Danzig came under the Prussian king. Recognized as a Free City by Napoleon in 1807, Danzig again became Prussian in 1814, and was from 1816 to 1824 and 1878 to 1920 the capital of the province of West Prussia. On November 15, 1920, the city was separated from the German Reich through the Versailles Treaty and, along with sections of the surrounding districts,was under the League of Nations as a Free State. Roughly 408,000 inhabitants lived in the approximately 1.966 km region, of which 90% were German.

[2]   Albert Forster was born in Fürth on July 26, 1902. As an apprentice he was enthused about Nationalism, and on his own initiative he established a local group in his home city. In 1930 Hitler appointed him representative of the NSDAP in the *Reichstag*, and in 1933 *Gauleiter* of Danzig. On October 5, 1939, the appointment to *Gauleiter* of Danzig and West Prussia followed. As a member of the SWS Forster reached the rank of *SS-Obergruppenführer*. After the war he was sentenced to death by a Polish court and executed.

[3]   At the same time the desire was already expressed for an exterritorial autobahn from Pomerania through the Polish corridor to Danzig.

The political course changed when, after the German occupation of Bohemia and Moravia, the English prime minister stated on March 31, 1939, in the House of Commons that England was ready to assist Poland in the event of a similar threat. Hitler actually had plans[4] formulated on how the military occupation of Danzig and its integration into the Reich, if possible, could take place without armed conflict. With the key phrase "Stolpmünde transport practice," it was planned that German aerial forces should be placed in Danzig in order to unite with the advancing German troops from East Prussia. The local units had to secure the Free City until the air landing.[5]

For these local units, it was a case of the already established *Einwohnerwehr*,[6] who strengthened the *Schutzpolizei* conceded by the League of Nations, as well as the barracked *Landespolizei*. The latter was established on Hitler's order from June 11, 1939. The acting *1. Generalstabsoffizier* Kurt Fetter later wrote:[7]

"Berlin, May 1939 - For us young Hauptleute *and students of the* Kriegsakademie, *the first year of our course of studies is coming to an end. That is why on one afternoon we sat together in the mess of the* Kriegsakademie *in order to prepare a lecture hall paper. Suddenly, I was called to the telephone, and received the order to report immediately to the head of the* Generalstab *of the army.... Shortly thereafter, for the first time in my life I entered the Bendlerblock, and reported to General Halder.[8] He led me to a table, and explained with the cards laying there the current deployment of Polish forces around Danzig, and their anticipated deployment against Danzig in the case of a military development. Subsequently, he informed me that for the protection of the Free City of Danzig against*

---

[4]   The completed *Geheime Kommandosache Fall Weiss* (Case White) on April 3, 1939, defined the duties of the *Wehrmacht* for an aggressive disruption of Poland.

[5]   At the same time, Poland ordered the mobilization that came to an end on August 27, 1939.

[6]   Dr. Heinz-Georg Migeod was trained in this in 1934:
"I come from the Strasburg district in Kulmerland but went to the Grundschule *and the* Realgymnasium *in Zoppot. An old* Feldwebel *in the brickyard behind the* Gymnasium *trained us 'volunteers' under the* Sekundaner *for the* Einwohnerwehr. *That was the first and gladly received breath of military life. In 1936 I went to the* Artillerie-Regiment 12 *in Schwerin as* Fahnenjunker, *from where I then reported to the* Luftwaffe *in 1938."*

[7]   Fett, Kurt: *Die Aufstellung der Gruppe Eberhardt*, in: *Beiträge zur Geschichte der 60. Infanterie-Division (mot.) spatter Panzergrenadier-Division Feldhermhalle*, o. O., 1979.

[8]   Franz Halder was born in Würzburg on June 30, 1884. On June 30, 1902, he entered the military as a *Fahnenjunker*, and was appointed to *Leutnant* in the *3. Fußartillerie-Regiment* on March 9, 1904. Appointed to *Oberstleutnant* on February 1, 1929, the promotion to *Oberst* followed on December 1, 1931, and the appointment to *Generalmajor* on July 1, 1934. On October 1, 1935, he commanded the *7. Division*, and one year later went to the *Generalstab* of the army. Promoted to *Generalleutnant* on August 1, 1936, and to *General der Artillerie* on February 1, 1938, he was as of August 27, 1938, the head of the *Generalstab* of the army. On July 19, 1940, the soldier honored with the Knight's Cross on October 27, 1939, was appointed to *Generaloberst*; however, he was dismissed in September 1942 due to differences with Hitler.

the feared Polish attacks, Hitler decided on the immediate formation of a Kampfgruppe *in this city, and reconciled with the political leadership of the Free City. The* Kampfgruppe *should reach—depending on options examined at the location—at least the strength of a reinforced* Infanterie-Regiment, *preferably, however, of a reinforced Brigade, that reports to the* Wehrkreiskommando I.

Generalmajor *Eberhardt,[9] now* Kommandeur *of an* Infanterie-Regiment *in East Prussia, will be in command of this* Kampfgruppe, *and be responsible for the execution of their deployment, effective immediately. I have been chosen as* Ia, *and shall verbally inform* Generalmajor *Eberhardt of the particulars....*

Having arrived in Danzig, we moved into quarters in Hotel Danziger Hof. Immediately on the next day we began with visits and meetings with the authorities and agencies that came into question. We were soon able to set up and move into our offices in the Wieben barracks. Later we moved into the Langfuhr barracks.

As a result of our meetings, the senate of the Free City of Danzig determined the necessary laws. The corresponding authorities enacted the necessary ordinances in order to legalize the prospective formation of a Landespolizei *in the form of a Brigade.[10]"*

On July 24, 1939, the senate of the Free City of Danzig ordered the formation of the *Landespolizei-Regimenter I* and *II*, and to each three detachments. The soldiers were citizens of Danzig, who partly served, or still served in the *Wehrmacht* in the Reich (mostly in East Prussia). *Die Technische Hochschule* Danzig placed the personnel, above all for the *Nachrichteneinheiten* and *Pioniereinheiten*.[11] In addition, the reinforced

---

[9]   Friedrich-Georg Eberhard was born in Straburg (Elsa) on January 15, 1892, and entered military service on March 11, 1910, as *Fahnenjunker*. On September 10, 1911, he was appointed to *Leutnant* in the *Dragoner-Regiment 6*. As of October 1, 1934, after his time in the *Reichswehr* he commanded the *Infanterie-Regiment 44* as *Oberst*. The promotion to *Generalmajor* took place on April 1, 1939. In May 1939 he took over the formation of a *Brigade* in Danzig that was formed within the *Landespolizei*. As of October 1, 1939, the appointment to *Kommandeur* of the *60. Infanterie-Division (mot.)*, which developed from the *Brigade* Eberhardt, followed. After the promotion to *Generalleutnant* on February 1, 1941, he took over the *38. Infanterie-Division* on June 30, 1942. At the command of the *174. Reserve-Division* in September 1943, in August 1944 the leadership of the *286. Sicherungs-Division* followed. Eberhardt was honored with the Knight's Cross.

[10]   On September 1, 1939, the Brigade Eberhardt was divided into:
-    the *Kommandostab* (*Kdr. Generalmajor* Eberhardt)
-    the *Landespolizei-Regiment I* (*Kdr. Oberst* Krappe)
-    the *Landespolizei-Regiment II* (*Kdr. Oberst* von Groddeck)
-    the *Artillerie-Abteilung* (*Kdr. Major* von Schön-Angerer)
-    the *Pionier-Kompanie* (Head: *Hauptmann* d. R. Stahlberg)
-    the *Nachrichten-Kompanie* (Head: *Leutnant* d. R. Schwenkhagen)
-    the *Versorgungs-Einheiten* (Head: *Hauptmann* d. R. Schlichting)

[11]   A physical examination had been conducted on June 2, 1939. On 4 July the induction into the *Landespolizei* followed; the service was initially held in civilian clothes. A later member of the *SS-Heimwehr Danzig* who studied at TH Danzig remembers:
"The Germans who were stationed in Danzig, who were conceived as reservists, were informed by a concealed Wehrbezirkskommando *at the German consulate general that they were permitted to leave the area of the Free*

Grenzaufsichtsdienst (VGAD)[12] formed from the SA men was incorporated into both *Landespolizei-Regimenter* with the strength of approximately 1,000 men. Along with this *Wehrmacht* unit—officially named *Landespolizei*—Himmler, as *Reichsführer-SS*, planned to establish a military contingent in Danzig. Hereby, two reasons were crucial:

1. he wanted access to Danzig citizens eligible for entry
   into the SS[13]
2. for propagandistic reasons, he wanted to participate in the
   incorporation of Danzig into the Reich.

Because a formation with recruits who had not served was impossible on short notice, and Himmler did not want to experience a fiasco with the foreseeable mission for reasons of prestige, he decided to command an SS unit to Danzig from the Reich, and reinforce it with citizens of Danzig. For this already existing SS unit, it involved the *III. Sturmbann* of the *4. SS-Totenkopf-Standarte* Ostmark.[14]

City of Danzig with the permission of this authority. The induction took place later – I no longer remember the time of the occurrence – with a letter that was worded roughly as follows:
On account of the law for the protection of the Free City of Danzig – it was quite equal to the protective law in the German Reich – you will be called into service with the Einwohnerwehr *of the Free City of Danzig.*"
On July 21, 1939, the SS arrested the student leader, Blume, because the majority of the students refused to report to the *SS-Heimwehr Danzig.*

[12]   Since 1935 the Danzig SA consisted of the *SA-Brigade 6* (*SA-Brigadeführer* Hacker) with the *SA-Standarten 5, 14*, and *128*, as well as the *SA-Reiter-Standarte 6*. From these units the *SA-Grenzwacht-Batallion* Hacker was formed on July 1, 1939. It was comprised of two *Schützen-Kompanien*, 1 *Nachrichten-*, and 1 Reiterzug, and was deployed primarily in September 1939 at the combing of the Oxhöfter Kämpe for dispersed Polish soldiers. At the same time, the reinforced border patrol duty was established under the commando of *SA-Obersturmbannführer* Jäger. Initially consisting of 400 members of the *SA-Standarte 5*, until September 1, 1939, the VGAD grew to approximately 1,000 men. The scope of duties ranged from the safeguarding of the borders against possible Polish invasions to enemy reconnaissance and opposing intelligence service on the observation of all occurrences on the other side of the border, collecting enemy reports, the guard of the finished and prepared barriers, to the possible blasting and occupying of lines of resistance. While the *SA-Grenzwacht-Batallion* Hacker was clothed in field gray, the members of the VGAD performed service predominantly in their brown SA uniforms. In addition to this existed the *Küstenschutz* Danzig, formed from the rows of the *SA-Marinesturmbann* that possessed the strength of approximately 220 members, as well as the *SA-Polizei-Hilfsdienst* with approximately 250 men.

[13]   This SS ability was given when the potential SS man did not have any physical flaws, such as visual, cardiac, or lung defects, varicose veins, hernia, or flat feet. Generally the height could not fall short of 1.72 m—for the *Leibstandarte Adolf Hitler* 1.78. Those previously convicted of criminal offenses (for example, property crimes or sex crimes) were likewise excluded.

[14]   As of April 1, 1938, the *Standarte* was deployed in the socalled Ostmark (Austria) with the peace location Steyr for the guard of the Mauthausen concentration camp. During the mobilization in the year 1939 the renaming to *SS-Totenkopf-Standarte 4* and the preparation for use as an occupation army followed. In November of the same year the regiment relocated to Prague, and in May 1940 to Holland. Hereby, the *I. Sturmbann* moved into the Hague, the *II. Sturmbann* into Groningen, and the newly formed *III. Sturmbann* into the Hertogenbosch quarter. As of August 26, 1940, Scheveningen appointed the units to coastal defense under the commander of the *Waffen-SS Nordwest*. On February 25, 1941, the transfer of the SS-*Totenkopf-Verband* into the *Waffen-SS* as SS-*Infanterie-Regiment 4* followed and mission within the *2. SS-Infanterie-Brigade* by Leningrad. In December 1941 the unit was ordered to Krakau in order to stand by as the third regiment for the *SS-Division Reich*. However, due to the development of the situation of the *Heeresgruppe Mitte* the members never came to Kaluga and Juchnow. On April 20, 1942, the regiment came together with 180 men, received the name Langemarck, and thereupon

After the German invasion of the Sudetenland in October 1938, Himmler ordered the *Schutzstaffel* to be reinforced by young, suitable Sudeten-Germans. This was to form a third *Sturmbann* (Batallion) within the 4. SS-*Totenkopf*[15]-*Standarte Ostmark*. One of them was Franz Pavlitcek:

"I was born during the last year of the First World War, and spent my youth—after the Versailles Treaty—as a person of German origin in Czechoslovakia. Aside from the different legislation of taxes, in our small area not much had changed. In 1938 the village still consisted exclusively of Germans. In our town's district it was different: 60% were Czechs, and 40% Germans. But the Czech state was not interested in our little village because there was only farming.

After attending the Bürgerschule *I initially worked in an office, which was no fun for me, so in 1934/35 I learned the profession of an electrician in a large factory.*

When I was then to be conscripted to the Czech army, I did not enlist, so the Czechs searched for me at home. Meanwhile, I hid myself in my work office. In August 1938, after it became more and more dangerous, I went with others, who were to be likewise mobilized by the Czech state, to the Grüner Kader *in the forest. There we were provided with food, and the latest news from our families.*

When the German Wehrmacht *then came into the Sudetenland, there was tremendous joy among the German population. The Czechs who, for example, lived in our town's district Hohenstadt became uneasy and moved away; however, some came back when it became calmer.*

A short time later the gymnastics club received the call to come to Miritz for an event. Because I was a member of such a club, I went along. When we—approximately 1,500 young Sudeten-Germans—arrived at the market square, someone walked around and examined us: this one, this one, this one, and this one.... We absolutely did not know what it was about, and that who was going through the ranks was Reichsführer-SS *Himmler. After the others stepped down, it was only we who stood, singled out. Our particulars were taken down, and it was said that we would receive a mobilization order within the next days.*

For this reason, on November 9, 1938, I then had to go to assembly in Mährisch-Neustadt, roughly 40km away. It was there I also learned that I was to join the Schutzstaffel, *which was an unknown entity to me at the time.*

---

formed the *SS-Schützen-Regiment* Langemarck on the Fallingbostel military training area. In 1943 the regiment was disbanded.

[15]   In 1938 Hitler declared that "*the* SS-Totenkopfverbände... *were neither a part of the* Wehrmacht *nor the police. They are a standing armed troop of the SS to help resolve special assignments of a police nature that I reserve to position case-by-case.*
As such and as a formation of the NSDAP they are to be ideologically and politically chosen according to the guidelines given by me to the NSDAP and the Schutzstaffeln, *to be trained and to be completed through the employment of SS able-bodied volunteers who satisfied their conscription into the* Wehrmacht...*"*

On November 14, 1938, I arrived in Oranienburg with other Sudeten-Germans.[16] *In the barracks grounds that were outside of the concentration camp we found accommodations in a bowling alley for approximately one week. We were informed quite quickly by our superiors where we were located. For us Sudeten-Germans this had been unknown. At the end of November 1938—still in civilian clothes—we were brought to Adlershof in a truck. There we received a white drill uniform, a black dress uniform, and a brown service uniform. I was assigned to the* 12./4. SS-Totenkopf-Standarte Ostmark. *I think that approximately 90% of the* III. Sturmbann *consisted of Sudeten-Germans...."*

Another was Bruno Fixl, who was already residing in Berlin in 1938:

"I was born in 1919, and grew up in Teplitz-Schönau. My father was a railway official, and was ultimately dismissed from duty because he refused to learn Czech. Because we were short on everything due to my father's unemployment, we received support through the Sudeten-German party.

I learned to be a confectioner, and before my conscription into the Czech Army in the middle of 1937 I took off for Berlin. I then worked in a bakery in Oranienburg. In 1938, along with other Sudeten-Germans in Berlin, I reported to the Sudetendeutsches Freikorps. *Because I was not accepted, and finally heard of the formation of the* III./4. SS-Totenkopf-Standarte Ostmark, *I reported there. The quarters in Berlin-Adlershof were in a desolate state, so we moved to Oranienburg. As of November 1, 1938, the first German recruits arrived. I was the first Sudeten-German in the* 4. Kompanie.

In mid-November the first transport with volunteers came from the Sudetenland, who were initially accommodated in a bowling alley.

The first Arbeitskommandos *then drove to Adlershof with armored personnel carriers in order to repair the greatest damages. At the end of the month the relocation took place, and for single groups the work began of making their rooms livable.*

During this time the second transport with Sudeten-Germans arrived, who were spread out on the single trains. Training on the heavy machine guns and carbines, sharp shooting, and diverse marches—also during the night—lasted until summer 1939. Shortly before the Danzig volunteers came to Adlershof, our entire Batallion*was located at the Döberitz military training area for a week."*

SS-Obersturmbannführer Hans-Friedmann Goetze[17] was appointed to *Kommandeur* of the *III. Sturmbann*, newly formed in Berlin-Adlershof. In addition to the approximately

---

[16]   The *2. SS-Totenkopf-Standarte* Brandenburg was located here.

[17]   Hans-Friedemann Goetze was born in Rendsburg on November 3, 1897. After attending the *Gymnasium* (*Primareife*) he joined the *2. Rekruten-Depot* of the *I. (ErsatzBatallion)/Infanterie-Regiment 31* as *Fahnenjunker* on February 1, 1915. Interrupted by a stay in a military hospital and service in o. g. *ErsatzBatallion*, he was— promoted to *Leutnant* on January 8, 1916—in the war in the *Infanterie-Regiment 31*. On December 27, 1918, he came to Mitau to the *Eiserne Division*, and served as of January 8, 1919, with the *Grenzschutz-Regiment 210*. In

500 Sudeten-Germans, roughly 100 citizens of the German Reich received their detail to a new formation. Willi Oswald was one of them:

"Due to the poor working conditions, I decided to enter the Schutzstaffel *in 1938. With a four-year period of duty I served as of November 1, 1938, in the* SS-Totenkopf-Verbände. *At the time I did not recognize any difference between this and the socalled* SS-Verfügungstruppe.
Even at home in Berlin I initially came to Oranienburg, and was evaluated once again. After approximately 6 weeks of training—still without weapons—I came to Adlershof to the 12./4. SS-Totenkopf-Standarte Ostmark *in December of the same year."*

From June 1939 on, this *III. Sturmbann*, whose original assignment was in the joint guard of the Mauthausen concentration camp,[18] formed the basis of the *SS-Heimwehr Danzig*.[19] Already in May 1939 the SS began to recruit volunteers for an *Einwohnerwehr* in Danzig— above all in the NS organizations, such as the *Hitlerjugend* and *Allgemeine Schutzstaffel*. It is interesting that the young men, as well as many of the previous Sudeten-Germans, apparently did not know that they were to come into the *Schutzstaffel*. Only the term *Einwohnerwehr* was spoken of. Primarily based on a physical selection, roughly 500 citizens of Danzig were accepted—no more had reported. While roughly 250 volunteers received training in Danzig, the other approximately 250 recruits came to Berlin-Adlershof. Kurt Enns was one of them:

"The registration office for the new recruits to the Einwohnerwehr *was located, of all places, in an SS-office in the Melzergasse, a branch of Langen Markt. Actually, I had expected uniformed police officers, because the* Einwohnerwehr *known to me was under the control of the* Schutzpolizei. *Instead what met us enrollees were those uniformed in*

1920 he belonged to the *Infanterie-Regiment 5* and—appointed to *Oberleutnant* on July 31, 1925—participated in various courses. After the promotion to *Hauptmann* on April 1, 1932, he withdrew from military service on January 31, 1933, and joined the SS with the rank of *SS-Hauptsturmführer*. Here he was appointed to *SS-Sturmbannführer* on September 12, 1937, and one year later to *SS-Obersturmbannführer*. From August 22 to September 17, 1938, he participated as *Hauptmann* a. D. d. R. in a drill in the *Beurlaubtenstande* with the *5./Infanterie-Regiment 61* Munich, and was appointed as of February 1, 1939, to *Major* of the Reserves in the *Beurlaubtenstande*. At the same time he took over the *III./4. Totenkopf-Standarte Ostmark* as *SS-Obersturmbannführer*. After the assignment as head of the *Sturmbann* Goetze (*SS-Heimwehr Danzig*) he led the *SS-Totenkopf-Infanterie-Regiment 3*. As its *Kommandeur* he fell at Le Paradis at 1520 hours on May 27, 1940. Goetze was honored on February 18, 1916, with the Iron Cross 2nd Class, on June 5, 1918, with the Wounded Badge in Black, and on November 31, 1918, with the Hamburg Hanseatic Cross. In the Second World War he received the clasp to the Iron Cross 2nd Class, as well as the Danzig Cross 1st and 2nd Class on September 26, 1939. Shortly before his death he was finally awarded the Iron Cross 1st Class.

[18]   Officially formed for the guarding of a concentration camp, however—due to the war-like organization—at the outset it seemed that the plan existed to form a potential reinforcement of the *SS-Verfügungstruppe*. By Hitler's instructions, the *Schutzstaffel*, with regard to the *Wehrmacht*, was to be permitted to establish a three regiment strong *Verfügungstruppe* as "*sole weapons carrier of the nation.*"

[19]   At this point in time discussion was only of a special assignment. The *Sturmbann* was initially named *Sturmbann* Goetze—the name "*SS-Heimwehr Danzig*" was first officially used at the presentation of the flag on August 18, 1939, on the Maifeld in Danzig.

black, mixed with some civilians. The rush was intense. Each of us wanted to protect our home.

Initially a medical screening took place. Anyone who did not pass this soon came out with a disappointed expression. If anyone approached him about what was happening inside, he received the simple answer, 'they didn't take me.' Finally, the time came when it was my turn. As the examining doctor asked for the usual requests—'left leg up, right leg up, what is your profession, do you have medical conditions, etc.'—and was satisfied with the overall result, he sent me into a second room, in which particulars were taken down, and further measurements and examinations were undertaken. I had passed and was physically fit.

On Friday, June 16, 1939, I was then called up, and had to report two days later at the same location at 1400 hours with marching rations and everything that was most important, for example: a toothbrush, soap, etc. When I reached the Melzergasse at the specified time, a truck was already there fully loaded with young men. Just as many volunteers waited next to it for their transport. Soon we drove through the Halbe-Allee, Langfuhr, and Olivia, and finally arrived in Zoppot. The open truck traveled with such speed that our hair was standing on end. It immediately went to the landing location at the outermost end of the landing stage—but it was difficult, as a large number of onlookers, primarily relatives and acquaintances of fellow passengers, and of my new comrades, blocked the way. At the top of the landing stage, the passenger ship Tannenberg *was anchored from Seedienst Ostpreußen. We were held back here so long from continuing our journey that, as soon as our last comrade was on board, the ship immediately cast off. From a greater distance we sailed around the Hela peninsula—with the magnificent sunshine and the calm sea, the journey was a summerly experience.*

For many of us it was the first journey outside of the Free State of Danzig—as it was for me. Soon the last landmarks of Danzig vanished on the horizon, and further along the Pomeranian coast the Tannenberg *headed for its destination, Swinemünde.*

When the ship headed for the gulf around morning with sirens wailing, we awoke in our hammocks. From the railing we looked out to the nearing port. An express train was already waiting there to go to Berlin. Two wagons were reserved for us. Those in black uniforms finally took charge of us. I could not let go of the feeling that we were not going to our intended Einwohnerwehr *at all...."*

Leo Wilm learned of the *Einwohnerwehr* in the *Allgemeine-SS*:

"Because I—born in 1919—had no desire to serve with the Schutzpolizei *in Danzig, and was already with the* Allgemeine-SS *in the Motorsturm there, I voluntarily joined a screening for the* SS-Verfügungstruppe *in March 1939. The result was I was fit for the* Leibstandarte Adolf Hitler.

My friend Georg Preuß,[20] *who was later honored with the Knight's Cross, was also present at this screening. We were both proud that we made it then, because from the approximately 30 of those gathered only we were eligible for the* LAH. *For us it was an honor. In October 1939 I was to be called in—Georg Preuß had been conscripted somewhat earlier.*

The political situation yielded that I was already a soldier before then, because an Einwohnerwehr *was to be formed in Danzig by us. I learned of this from* SS-Sturmbannführer *Ristau in the* Allgemeine-SS. *He knew of my enrollment into the* LAH, *and asked me if I would go to the* Einwohnerwehr *regardless. I affirmed this with the condition that the matter had to be resolved by October. He responded, 'by then everything will have been forgotten.' How horrible was his prognosis....''*

Herbert Schönfeld was likewise a volunteer for the *Einwohnerwehr:*

"In May 1939 I had already finished my apprenticeship as a lumber merchant, and was then Scharführer *in the* Hitlerjugend. *At a meeting of the leaders, the then* Stammführer *or* Bannführer *said to us that a* Freikorps *was being established in Danzig, and for each of us it would be a matter of course to voluntarily report. So with an HJ comrade I went to Danzig-Langfuhr to a villa in the Halbe-Allee. There bustling activity reigned. The rooms were teeming with young people. Shortly after taking down particulars a prescreening began. Doctors for general medicine, eye specialists, and ears, nose, and throat specialists carried out the examinations. After this procedure a letter was thrust in my hands with the following contents:*

'For the purpose of fulfilling your official duty in the Einwohnerwehr Danzig *you must report in Danzig, Melzergasse, on Sunday, June 18, 1939, at 1400 hours. Bring provisions for one day, as well as something to clean your teeth and shoes.'*

So I received my call-up orders, so to speak, to the Einwohnerwehr Danzig, *and waited for my comrade Horst Frisch. He finally arrived; however, in low spirits, and told me that he was not accepted. Naturally, I asked him for what reason, and he said because of 'drooping shoulders.' I was very disappointed, and also didn't want to go any longer. But one of the doctors said to me 'Boy, you will get to know many more comrades.' And so it was, as well.*

On Sunday, June 18, 1939, I marched with my small package under my arm to Melzergasse in Danzig. Different trucks from various firms were ready there, and brought us to Zoppot after a tour through Danzig's city center. On the way there was much singing—the atmosphere was tremendous on the vehicles. A ship from Seedienst Ostpreußen was at the landing stage in Zoppot. We climbed from our vehicles onto the ship and sailed to Swinemünde. On the ship we received 5 Reichmarks so that we could buy ourselves something to eat, as well. From Swinemünde we took the train to Berlin-Adlershof. Here I realized that I had arrived at the SS....''

---

[20]   Georg Preuß received the Knight's Cross on February 25, 1945, as *SS-Obersturmführer* and *Führer* of the *10. (gep.)/SS-Panzergrenadier-Regiment 2 LSSAH.*

Kurt Rodde remembers similarly:

"On May 13, 1921, I was born in East Prussia. In 1923 my mother moved with us four children to Gr. Mausdorf (Gr. Werder district), into the Free State of Danzig. In Kalthof I learned the profession of an engine fitter, and was a member of the Motor-HJ. *During a social evening we were asked to participate in the rallying for an* Einwohnerwehr *for the protection of the Free City of Danzig on June 14, 1939. Already on the next day I was called up for an indefinite period, and drove in a truck with approximately 10 volunteers to Zoppot, and from the landing stage to Swinemünde with a ship from the Seedienst Ostpreußen. On the ship men in black uniforms instructed us. The particulars were taken again, and some money was disbursed.*

Wolfgang Grönke likewise wanted to go to the *Heimwehr*:

"My friend Eberhard Rohde and I in the Wieben barracks wanted to voluntarily report to the Einwohnerwehr. *One sent us home; we (both born in 1923) were to be patient. We were disappointed.*
However, we later paid for our then war fever, aside from the loss of our homes, with injuries and 5 years of Soviet war captivity...."

In Berlin-Adlershof, roughly 250 citizens of Danzig reinforced the *III./4. SS-Totenkopf-Standarte*, and were distributed to various groups. Erwin Richert remembers the days in Berlin:

"From the Zoppot landing stage we sailed in the ship Hansestadt Danzig[21] *to Swinemünde, and from there to Berlin-Adlershof for basic training. On the way we saw a plane crash; the pilot was saved by a* Schnellboot *of the Navy. Our* Kompaniechef SS-Obersturmführer *Schultz was in Adlershof. For our first time on pass our* Kompanie *was led closed to the barracks gate. We walked in single groups in the city. Our first destination was Potsdam, later Berlin."*

Herbert Schönfeld remembers:

"In Adlershof we were accommodated in barracks, and initially began training in our civilian clothes. Gradually the outfitting was also carried out. In addition to the field gray

---

[21]   The *Seedienst Ostpreußen*, utilized as a minelayer from the beginning of the war under *Korvettenkapitän* Wilhelm Schröder, and formerly a seaside excursion steamboat of reknown, was deployed in 1940 with a *Husarenstück*. On 7 April of the same year the ship headed for the Travenmünde port, and was secured at the socalled Ostpreußenkai. Under night's protection approximately 1,000 soldiers of the *198. Infanterie-Division* went on board below deck with light weapons, 150 bikes, and 5 motorcycles. The dumbfounded team explained to Schröder that it concerned a filming for a Navy film.
In fact, Operation Kassel was underway, with which Copenhagen was to be occupied. At 0515 hours on April 8, 1940, the Hanseatic City Danzig landed in the Copenhagen port. The members of the *198. Infanterie-Division* came onto land and occupied important military sites *"as friends for the protection of the Danish neutrality from English attacks"* (sic!). Without any losses, the Danish capital was occupied. At 1445 hours the Hanseatic City Danzig left the port and went to Warnemünde in order to proceed to Bornholm from there on April 10, 1940. This island was also smoothly occupied.

and drill uniforms, we also received the black uniform. Steel helmets, carbines, bayonets, and knapsacks—everything that a "prospective soldier" would need. And rigorous military training over and over. In the morning at 0400 hours we awoke, and if the UvD was gracious, we could finally collapse into bed at 2200 hours. After six weeks we went back to Danzig on the ship."

As well as the *III./4. SS-Totenkopf-Standarte* and the Danzig volunteers serving as the stem, other *SS-Totenkopf* units reinforced the *SS-Heimwehr Danzig*. However, they did not transfer to Berlin-Adlershof, but rather received the initial orders to Oranienburg. Otto Brabänder came from the *13./I. SS-Totenkopf Standarte Oberbayern*:

"I was born in the Palatinate on January 4, 1914, and was in the SA since 1928. From March 4 to 29, 1934, I attended the SA-Sportschule III Leichlingen, *and from January 6 to February 23 the* SA-Sportschule Deggingen. *I belonged to the* SA-Hilfswerk Kurpfalz *in the Horst-Wessel Barracks in Mainz from April 24 to October 31, 1935. From there I served in the* 13./Infanterie-Regiment 63 *in Ingolstadt until October 28, 1938. Influenced by the* Schutzstaffel *at the Nuremberg Rally in 1938, I joined them, and because I wanted to stay in the Ingolstadt area, I chose the* 1. SS-Totenkopf-Standarte Oberbayern *for my further service. On November 1938 I came to the* 13. Kompanie *there, and from there on May 12, 1939, over Oranienburg to Königsberg in the exhibition halls."*

Georg Diehl was detailed with the *14./1. SS-Totenkopf-Standarte Oberbayern* to the formation of the *SS-Heimwehr Danzig*:

"Already in June 1939 watchwords were emerging that a special mission was again up in the air. But no one knew what, where, or when. Then suddenly: 13. and 14. Kompanie *get ready to march.*
Then both Kompanien *marched separately, in the mot. march direction north on the autobahn. After a long, strenuous journey, Oranienburg was the first stage objective. Here our field gray and small arms were packed, and it continued in black uniform until in the port of Stettin,* Lütje-Hörn *(8,000 to.) were already ready to be loaded. After two days of sea travel we landed in Königsberg. The drivers remained on the freighter, and the team was sent from the white fleet of the* Seedienst Ostpreußen. *In Königsberg the vehicles were changed to civilian, and the guns and equipment were packed in large boxes. The teams then drove as* SS-Sportgemeinschaft Königsberg, Gumbinnen, Allenstein, *etc. to the* SS sports festival *in Danzig...."*

Hans Heins was a member of the newly formed *Kraftfahrsturm* of the *2. SS-Totenkopf-Standarte Brandenburg*:

"On June 19, 1939, with roughly 35 Unterführer *and men from the* Kraftfahrabteilung Oranienburg *(Head:* SS-Hauptsturmführer *Schneider) I sent the* Vorkommando *to Danzig.*

The journey initially led to Stettin into the free port area in a truck. The loading by the shipping company Yvers and Artl onto the Lütje-Hörn *followed. The ship drove on behalf of the Reich—the crew especially obliged. The journey proceeded along the Pomeranian coast to Königsberg, where on June 23, 1939 we arrived and unloaded. The unloading took place with the help of the shipping company. In Königsberg, the* Vorkommando *was provided with identification from the* Staatspolizei *for the* Ostpreußen-Danzig *small border traffic, and the vehicles were repaired. We were wearing civilian clothes, and accommodated in Königsberg with the* Pioniersturm *of the* Allgemeine-SS. *There we also received identification cards that made us residents of Danzig. We were brought to Danzig by means of KdF busses, while other waterways transferred weapons, munitions, guns, and trucks in small power gliders between Vistula Lagoon and the Vistula. Training then continued in Danzig immediately...."*

Hans Balzer belonged to the same unit, and remembers his path to the *SS-Heimwehr Danzig*:

"The endless marching with the 05/15 MG on my shoulder had put a damper on my 'Stoppelhopser enthusiasm.' Every Saturday we marched 30 km, then into exercises in Oranienburg – Rheinsberg – Wittstock – Röbel – Waren, to sharp shooting Stettin – Anklam, and 6 weeks Nuremberg Rally *from 6 in the morning. In October 1937 from Brieg to Glatz, from Appenweiler in the unfinished Westwall, from Zittau to Reichenberg – Gablonz, to Operation Hühnerwasser – Weisswasser, then to Bodenbach (Elbsandsteingebirge)—blood group tattooing ther—thereupon swearing-in in Munich, and finally vacation.*
The chaos on foot was enough; I wanted something more modern. Having just turned 18, I was offered to take a driving test; my Gruppenführer *became the sarge of the newly formed* Kraftfahrkompanie, *and I went along.*
The first driving lesson was behind the enormous steering wheel of a Büssing-Diesel M.T.W. across Berlin. The drive through ice and snow at the Czech occupation was strenuous and thrilling. Until then it had been quite a lot, and when we celebrated our Sturmmann *in April 1939, we did not suspect that we would be caught by a gust long before the storm that twirled us breathtakingly higher and higher, until after 6 years we abruptly crashed and almost broke our necks.*
And so it began: what is the world and Berlin worth with more money, new uniforms to go out in, and for the first time a night pass. To "Strahlauer Fischzug" and to the "Treptower Volksfest," very close to Berlin's bosom. Exhausted, we caught the last S-Bahn headed home. The Garnisonswache received us ambiguously: run, all hell has broken loose. In fact, everything was brightly illuminated, but deadly silent: all lockers empty, and all beds crossways and stripped. Already the UvD is hollering. All the vehicles are already out, we jump into the few remaining, and drive in a small column to the gate over Bernau to the new Stettin autobahn. There in the dark other vehicles greeted us, and by the first light of dawn the convoy drove by dumbfounded guards through the gate of the Stettin free port directly over ramps into the cellar of a large quay shelter. The accommodations were

temporary, the provisions from the shipping company better, and the best was the outings into the beautiful city halfway in civilian attire.
After several days we loaded onto the Lütje-Hörn, *and navigated approximately 18 hours on a calm sea, mostly below deck to Königsberg. There we pulled into a boathouse of the* Allgemeine-SS *on the Pregelinsel, and converted the vehicles to civilian. My truck received a claret color and the label 'Weinhandlung Krause.' In police headquarters we received identification and trip tickets for the small border traffic.*
During night missions together with the Elbinger Allgemeine-SS,, *the vehicles were ferried with a 'Handzugfähre' (rope ferry) over both Nogatdämme, and the motors were started far behind the embankment. Then we went without light until Tiegenhof, over further Käsemark into the Wieben barracks. Finally we landed in the gymnasium in Ohra."*

In order to explain the presence of approximately 1,500 SS men in Danzig to critical observers, a three-day SS Sport Festival—primarily with athletic disciplines—was started. As the socalled *SS-Sportgemeinschaften* from the entire Reich—but primarily from East Prussia—the members of the *SS-Heimwehr Danzig* came into the Free City. Kurt Enns describes the path of the *Schützenkompanien* from Berlin to Danzig:

"The way to the S-Bahn, that was roughly 1.5 km far from our Adlershof barracks camp, was the most difficult to manage. The suitcases became an almost unbearable burden. On one hand, the march formation had to be held to some degree, while on the other hand, one had to constantly take the heavy suitcases from one hand to the other. Short inserted breaks also could change little. When we finally arrived at the S-Bahn, the greatest exertions were over. The D-Zug to Swinemünde led us directly to the landing stage of the passenger ship Kaiser, *changed to* Seedienst Ostpreußen. *It was an older ship that, however, completely satisfied tourist traffic on the Baltic Sea.*
When we arrived in Zoppot, two pleasure steamers of the Danzig Weichsel AG were already waiting that brought us over Neufahrwasser by the Westerplatte to Danzig. Although none of us from Adlershof were permitted to report our arrival, a considerable crowd had gathered at the landing stage. With our heavy suitcases we marched to the exhibition hall that was on the Wallgasse. However, this was only a temporary stay until our accommodations in Matzkau were ready for occupancy...."

Immediately after the arrival in the Free City training resumed, and according to the original assignment, the defense positions were completed. Adalbert Meironke remembers:

"I lived in Oliva, corner Adolf-Hitler-Straße - Seestraße (direction of Glettkau). There, on the large Salzmann'schen Feld, the SS-Heimwehr *set up a system of trenches. It was said to us that it was for maneuver practice. I was then 13 years old and always nearby, like boys are. We lived directly across the way. My mother made coffee and food for the unit. These preparations were at many locations to Zoppot and elsewhere...."*

After a couple of days the *SS-Heimwehr* was assigned to their fixed quarters:

- the Wieben barracks, in which the other half of the Danzig volunteers were also trained
- the gymnasium in Ohre
- the buildings in Matzkau, which later became prison camps of the *Waffen-SS*
- the casemates at the Bischofsberg

The events in Danzig were not concealed from the attentive observers in Poland and other European states. The *Neue Zürcher Zeitung* No. 211 wrote on August 1, 1939:

"The Militarization of Danzig
The Berlin correspondent of the semi-official 'Gazeta Polksa' asserts in a lengthy report dated from Danzig on the militarization of Danzig, that the Free City has increased the strength of their Landespolizei *since the* Märzkrise[22] *from 1,000 to 4,500 men. The* Landespolizei *is organized into three Regiments, of which two are already established, while the third finds itself still in formation. The armament of these* Polizeiregimenter *corresponds to that of a German* Infanterieregiment. *In addition, eight thousand SS men, who for the most part have come from out of town, are located in Danzig; they are being accommodated in the former Prussian barracks, electric companies, schoolhouses, in the hall of the Danzig exhibition, and a gymnasium. The SS people were later relocated to Matzkau. All weapons were brought on the sea route from Hamburg and Stettin to Danzig. In this manner, the Free City has sufficient weapons for a* Tankkompanie, *obtained two to three batteries field artillery and heavy artillery, furthermore 36 anti-tank guns and numerous infantry guns."*

Already on the next day the *Schweiser Zeitung* reported:

"The militarization of Danzig – Concerns in London
Despite Chamberlain's assurance in his House of Commons speech last Monday that many newspaper reports on the remilitarization of Danzig are exaggerated, influential London circles follow the development of the situation and the military measures in the Free City with nervous attention. A factual list of Danzig's activities up until now in the 'Gazeta Polksa' received much attention, that, like the 'Times' commented, would not have appeared in this semi-official newspaper with such extensive details if the Polish government did not treat the situation with increasing concern. As a result of a report come into hand here it intends within the course of the next days to make a severe protest to the Danzig Senate. On the occasion of the 25th commemoration day of the march of the Pilsudsky-Legion against the Russian border, Marschall Ridz-Smigly[23] will presumably rewrite the disposition and

---

[22]   In March 1939 a crisis arose when England assured assistance to Poland for a similar case after the German invasion of Bohemia and Moravia, and Poland ordered a partial mobilization at the same time.

politics of Poland on the Danzig problem in more depth before a mass meeting. Today in a leading article the 'Daily Telegraph' will call attention to the constantly increasing tension in Danzig. Currently the armed forces in the Free City would include 15,000 men according to reliable estimates, of which at least half are Germans. It is not once concealed that for a long time artillery, tanks, and munitions have been imported in a public wounding of the Danzig status. The retreat of the Polish inspectors from the Danzig margarine factory, explains the 'Daily Telegraph,' must further complicate the situation that is already charged with explosive material, because it fosters the repeal of the customs union with Poland and the incorporation of Danzig into the Reich. Whether the German threat that thereupon follows serves as the strike designed to put pressure on Poland, such as what happened last year around this time against Czechoslovakia, remains to be seen. After Chamberlin reiterated on Monday his clear warnings from July 10, it is to hope, concludes 'Daily Telegraph,' that Berlin will give up its illusion regarding Danzig before it is too late to prevent a catastrophe."

Another report on the situation in Danzig can be read in the *"Neue Zürcher Zeitung"* on August 3, 1939:

"According to information from a reliable source and some observations of the representative of the 'United Press,' at this time Danzig has roughly 6,000 men in arms. The regular police armed forces add up to 1,000 men, to which 4,000 more are coming, who in the course of the last weeks were called in as 'police recruits.' In addition, 1,000 SS soldiers stand by, of which 600 form the 'Heimwehr,' while the rest find use as Police reserves. Furthermore, a troop of 8,000 SA people exists that occasionally are called on for voluntary service. The police and the SS are armed. In contrast, no weapons were distributed among the SA.
These defense forces of the Free State are equipped, as can be determined, with machine guns, small trench mortars, light anti-aircraft artillery, armored cars, and anti-tank artillery. It is quite difficult to determine the amount of the remaining armaments, and reliable information on the topic is not available."

Along with the hard service, the members of the *SS-Heimwehr Danzig* could organize their free time themselves. Bruno Fixl on the last days of peace:

"The 'structuring of leisure time' was one-time due to the cordiality of the Danzig population for our troop. In magnificent weather that prevailed then, Saturday afternoons and Sunday swimming excursions to the Baltic Sea, Heubude—the seaside resorts of the citizens of Danzig—were the main programs. However, the city also offered its beauties, and no one thought about war. If one had met Polish navy soldiers, there would have been smiling greetings...."

---

[23]   Marschall Rydz-Smigly (not Ridz-Smigly) was *Oberbefehlshaber* of the Polish armed forces.

Willi Oswald has similar memories:

"We had a dreamlike time in Danzig. Our troop provisions consisted daily of meat, potatoes, and vegetables!
If we were in our uniforms in a café or pub and wanted to pay for food and drinks, the server or host made a gesture of refusal, and said that someone had already paid for this for us...."

On August 17, 1939, the men received two stripes with the name *SS-Heimwehr Danzig* handed over, to sew one immediately for the next day onto the left sleeves of the field gray uniform blouse. The second stripe was intended for the black dress uniform. On Friday, August 18, 1939, the first official march of the *SS-Heimwehr* took place. Here the *Gauleiter* of Danzig, Albert Forster, presented the SS unit a flag. In front of 50,000 spectators he gave a speech typical of the time on the Maifeld:

"After the goodbye parade of all troop detachments that had been stationed in Danzig had taken place on January 22, 1920, the Leibhusaren *marched out on February 7, 1920, as the last of the German troops....*
Numerous tears were shed when the German troops moved out of this beloved garrison, and with this Danzig was abandoned to defenselessness....
Hence, no other option remains in this threatening situation, than to help ourselves. Every responsible state leadership, no matter what country, would not have done anything different than what we have done in the last eight weeks. We have seen to it that Danzig and its population are no longer defenseless. In such times, however immediate, dead letters from some kind of treaty or constitution are not decisive, but rather the instinct of self preservation of 400,000 men....
You, my comrades, are such a resistance organization, who are united in the SS-Heimwehr Danzig. *The name* Heimwehr *says everything by itself; you my young comrades have voluntarily reported over the past weeks even when told what was involved....*
As young citizens of Danzig, you did not want to stand aside when it comes down to protecting your own home. Within a short time you were trained. Your enthusiasm and the joyful dedication to it made it possible for you to become soldiers over the short span of a few weeks....
You, my comrades of the SS-Heimwehr Danzig, *can have the satisfaction that you are the first in nearly 20 years who have marched up to Danzig with such military gear. Only a flag is missing. The flag was at all times an emblem that waves ahead for the soldiers on good as well as on bad days. In the past, the flag was always the symbol around which the soldiers crowded. It will be the same in the future. The flag that I have the honor of presenting to you carries the symbols that must remain sacred and dear to you....*

I do not need to emphasize for you, my comrades, that with the flag is the highest standard that there is for you. The flag always tells of victory when it waves and flutters....
We will make sure that, in the future of our entire German people, that the flag with the swastika, *the symbol of light and the sun, waves ahead. No matter what may come, we will then always be the victors at the end.... I know, my comrades of the* SS-Heimwehr Danzig, *when I present your* Kommandeur *with the flag, that what I say to you, you will follow truly and faithfully...."*

In connection with this, *SS-Obersturmbannführer* Goetze held a speech —likewise quoted here in excerpts:

"Gauleiter, *my SS-comrades!*
Eight weeks since we were pulled here, since we were needed at home, we who in the Reich outside were active in units or professions....
Today for the first time this unit stands solid before our eyes. We know we are not fit for parades, like a finished troop must be, but we also don't want to make any parades. We want to fight...for that which is sacred to us.... We can say that sincerely and full of pride: today we are operational....
Today the last thing is given to us that we as soldiers desire: the flag, that should wave ahead for us, and that shows where the storm rages around us....
We want the oath that we pledge again and again at each service and daily activity, through which to express that we say: come what may, we will stand where our Führer *places us. There we will remain, and there we will not falter...."*

The quarters in Berlin-Adlershof.

Pentecost 1939 at the Döberitz military training area.

The first outing of the Danzig citizens in Berlin-Adlershof.

Training in Berlin - Adlershof

At machine gun.

Group photographs.

Training in Berlin - Adlershof

On march with MG 08/15.

Training on the sMG.

Practice with MG 08/15 in Berlin-Adlershof.

Training

Departure from Danzig to Berlin for training...

...and the return from Szczecin to Danzig.

Rest during the crossing.

Crossing

At the Königsberg harbor: men of the SS-HWD halfway dressed in civilian clothes observe the loading of the weapons.

The 3.7 PaK artillery, stored in boxes, are loaded onto small power gliders.

In the middle is *SS-Rottenführer* Pietsch, who was deployed in Danzig-Ohra as *Tankwart*.

Königsberg Port

With the Vistula ferry by Käsemark, Mercedes jeeps were picked up from Königsberg.

The mood is good.

At the landing stage.

Vistula ferry

Identification issued to the motorists in Königsberg.

The three-day SS Sport Festival in Danzig.

View above the roofs.

Langgassentor.

Artushof.

Cityscape of Danzig

Frauengasse and St. Marien.

Krantor.

Milchkannen Bridge and Gate.

From an album

Training at the barrack yard.

On duty.

At the barrack yard.

Wieben barracks Duty

Wearing method of the strip on the left underarm, here the team's design.

The stripes of the *SS-Heimwehr Danzig* were delivered to the soldiers on August 17, 1939, in dual style for the presentation of the flag on the next day.

Style for *SS-Führer*

Sleeve band of the *SS-Heimwehr Danzig*

From left to right: *SS-Obersturmbannführer* Goetze, *Gen.Majr.* Eberhardt, *Gauleiter* Forster, and *SS-Oberführer* Schäfer.

Parade of the *sMG-Kompanie* before *Gauleiter* Forster, *Gen. Maj.* Eberhardt, and *SS-Obersturmbannführer* Goetze.

Inspection of the SS-HWD by Gauleiter Forster.

Maifeld 8/18/39

Panzerabwehr-Kompanie

A Kompanie lines up.

Speech by SS-
Obersturmbannführer
Goetze.

Maifeld 6/16/39

The presentation of the flag.

The flag.

SS-Untersturmführer Zipp, *SS-Obersturmführer* Hilgenstock, and *SS-Untersturmführer.*

Presentation of the flag

Marching off from Maifeld.

The insert of the *Danziger Neueste Nachrichten* from 8/20/39.

Franz Pavlitcek

SS-Sturmmann Willi Oswald.

Kurt Rodde

Otto Brabänder

Men of the SS-Heimwehr Danzig

Identity card of the *SS-Heimwehr Danzig*.

Documents

War Missions

After the British assurance of assistance for Poland in March 1939, Hitler feared being involved in a potential conflict of a long-lasting war on two fronts. His efforts, therefore, amounted to coming to an arrangement with England in the west and the Soviet Union in the east in order to exclude an intervention of both powers in the case of war. In contrast to Great Britain, the ratification of the German-Soviet friendship and nonaggression pacts with Stalin finally came about in August 1939. Hitter had achieved what he wanted: due to the relationship with the UdSSR, and to the intervention of the Red Army in the forthcoming German-Polish conflict, he was convinced he would be able to conquer Poland in a few weeks, and thus prevent a war on two fronts.

On August 25, 1939, at 1502 hours Hitler gave the order to spark the *Fall Weiß* (Case White) for the next day, which he, however, called off at 1815 hours. After the failure of diplomatic efforts he then, on August 31, 1939, at 1240 hours decisively ordered the attack on Poland.

According to the operations plan, the *Heeresgruppe Süd* (*Generaloberst* von Rundstedt[24]) reported with the *10. Armee* (*General der Artillerie* von Reichenau[25]) from Schlesien to Nordosten on Warsaw, shielded in the south by the *14. Armee* (*Generaloberst* List[26]) in Slovakia, and in the north from the *8. Armee* (*General der Infanterie* Blaskowitz[27]). The

---

[24] Gerd von Rundstedt was born on December 12, 1875, in Aschersleben. He reported to military service as *Fähnrich* on March 22, 1982, and was *Leutnant* in the *Infanterie-Regiment 83* one year later. On November 1, 1927, he received the promotion to *Generalmajor*, and on March 1, 1929, to *Generalleutnant*. With the takeover of the *Gruppenkommando I* on October 1, 1932, von Rundstedt received the rank of *General der Infanterie*. On November 1, 1938, he withdrew from military service as *Generaloberst* (March 1, 1938); however, he took over the *Heeresgruppe Süd* in Summer 1939. On October 1, 1940, he was *Oberbefehlshaber West*, and commanded the *Heeresgruppe Süd* again from June 10, 1941, to December 1, 1942. As of March 15, 1942, he was *OB West*. Von Rundstedt, honored with the Knight's Cross with Oak Leaves and Swords, died in Hannover in 1953.

[25] Walter von Reichenau was born on October 1884 in Karlsruhe. He entered military service as *Fahnenjunker* on March 14, 1903, and was appointed to *Leutnant* in the *1. Garde-Fußartillerie-Regiment* on August 18, 1904. Promoted to *Generalleutnant* on October 1, 1935, he took over the *VII. Armee-Korps*, and after the appointment to *General der Artillerie* (October 1, 1936) the *Gruppenkommando 4* on March 1, 1938. In September 1939 he commanded the *10. Armee*, and took over command of the *6. Armee* on October 20, 1939. Promoted to *Generalfeldmarschal* on July 19, 1940, von Reichenau led the *Heeresgruppe Süd* as of December 1, 1941. On September 30, 1939, he was awarded the Knight's Cross. He died on January 17, 1942, after a stroke.

[26] Wilhelm List was born on May 14, 1880, in Oberkirch. He entered the army as *Fahnenjunker* on July 15, 1898, and was appointed on March 7, 1900, to *Leutnant* in the Bavarian *1. Pionier-Batallion*. On October 1, 1930, List was promoted to *Generalmajor*, and as *Generalleutnant* (October 1, 1932) led the *4. Division* as of October 1, 1933. With the promotion to *General der Infanterie* he took over the *IV. Armee-Korps* on October 1, 1935. On April 1, 1938, he was appointed as *Generaloberst* (April 1, 1937) to *Oberbefehlshaber* of *Gruppenkommando 5*. In September 1939 List commanded first the *14. Armee* and then the *12. Armee*. As *OB Südost* he was appointed *Generalfeldmarschall* (July 19, 1940) from July 1 until October 15, 1941. Finally, from July 10 until September 10, 1942, he led the *Heeresgruppe A*. List was honored with the Knight's Cross.

Heeresgruppe Nord (*Generaloberst* von Bock[28]) was to unite with the *3. Armee* (*General der Artillerie* von Küchler[29]) from East Prussia and the *4. Armee* (*General der Artillerie* von Kluge[30]) from Pomerania in the socalled Polish corridor, advance with the *3. Armee* toward the south, and there meet the *10. Armee*.

The Brigade Eberhardt and the *SS-Heimwehr Danzig* were placed under the command of the *3. Armee* already on August 25, 1939, and finally fought in and around Danzig.

---

[27]   Johannes Blaskowitz was born on July 10, 1883, in Peterswalde. On March 2, 1901, he entered the army as *Fähnrich*, and was appointed *Leutnant* in the *Infanterie-Regiment 18* on January 27, 1902. After the appointments to *Generalmajor* (October 1, 1931) and *Generalleutnant* (December 1, 1933), he took over supreme command of *Heeresgruppe 3* as *General der Infanterie* (August 1, 1936) on November 10, 1938. In September 1939 he initially led the *AOK 8*, and as of October of the same year—under promotion to *Generaloberst*—the *AOK 2*. From October 20, 1939, on he was deployed as *OB Ost*, and took over the *AOK 9* from May 14-29, 1940. *Militärbefehlshaber* for a short time in Northern France, he commanded the *AOK 1* from October 25, 1940, until May 3, 1944. After leading the *Armeegruppe G* in May 1944, and the transfer to *Führerreserve* of the *OKH* on September 21, 1944, he took over the *Heeresgruppe G* on 24 December of the same year, and roughly one month later the *Heeresgruppe H*. From April 7 until May 5, 1945, he was *OB Niederland Befehlshaber* of the *Stronghold of Holland*. Blaskowitz, honored with the Knight's Cross Oak Leaves and Swords, committed suicide on February 5, 1948, in an Allies Nuremberg war criminal prison.

[28]   Fedor von Bock was born on December 3, 1880, in Küstrin. In 1898 he served in the *5. Garde-Regiment* on foot. *Stabsoffizier* in the First World War, after 31 years of service he received in the *Reichswehr* on February 1, 1929, the rank of *Generalmajor*. The promotion to *Generalleutnant* was declared on February 1, 1931, and to *General der Infanterie* on March 1, 1935. Promoted to *Generaloberst* on March 1, 1938, he was, as of 10 November of the same year, *Oberbefehlshaber* of the *Heeresgruppenkommando I*. As of August 26, 1939, he led the *Heeresgruppe Nord*. The command of *Heeresgruppe B* followed on October 3, 1939, and the *Heeresgruppe Mitte* on April 1, 1941. In December of the same year von Bock was accepted into the *Führerreserve* of the *OKH*. After the leadership of the *Heeresgruppe Süd* from January 16 until July 13, 1942, he withdrew and stood at the disposal of the supreme commander of the *Wehrmacht*. On September 30, 1939, he was honored with the Knight's Cross, and fell as *Generalfeldmarschall* (July 19, 1940) on May 3, 1945, in Schleswig-Holstein during a British air attack.

[29]   Georg von Küchler was born on May 30, 1881, in Schloß Philippsruh. He entered military service as *Fahnenjunker* on March 12, 1900, and was appointed to *Leutnant* in the *Feldartillerie-Regiment 25* on August 18, 1901. After his assignment during the First World War and time in the *Reichswehr*, he reached the rank of a *Generalmajor* on April 1, 1934. On December 1, 1935, the appointment to *Generalleutnant* followed. With the promotion to *General der Artillerie* on April 1, 1937, von Küchler took over the command of the *I. Armee-Korps*. At the beginning of the war he commanded the *3. Armee* and, as of 5 November of the same year the *18. Armee*. From January 17, 1942, to January 1944 he was *Oberbefehlshaber* of the *Heeresgruppe Nord*. He was awarded with the Knight's Cross on September 30, 1939, and on August 21, 1943, with the Oak Leaves.

[30]   Günter von Kluge was born on October 30, 1882, in Posen, and served on March 22, 1901, in the *Feldartillerie-Regiment 46*. On February 1, 1933, he was appointed to *Generalmajor* and, as of 1 October of the same year functioned as inspector of the *Nachrichtentruppen*. Promoted to *Generalleutnant* on April 1, 1934, half a year later he commanded the *6. Division*. As of April 1, 1935, he was the commanding *General* of the *VI. Armee-Korps*, and was appointed to *General der Artillerie* on August 1, 1936, in this official position. After having supreme command of the *Gruppenkommando 6* (December 1, 1938) he took over the *4. Armee* in August 1939, and after the promotion to *Generaloberst* (October 1, 1939) the *Heeresgruppe Mitte* on December 19, 1941, as *Generalfeldmarschall* (July 19, 1940). From July 2, 1944, on von Kluge commanded the *Heeresgruppe D*—as of July 19, 1944, also the *Heeresgruppe B* in personal union—and was *OB West*. The General, honored with the Knight's Cross with Oak Leaves and Swords, committed suicide in August 1944.

The Battle for the Polish Post Office

The Polish post office at Heveliusplatz was the former Danzig garrison military hospital, and correspondingly was built robustly. Given to the Poles for use as a post office, they additionally reinforced the building in the pursuit of a fixed stronghold in the city. As postal service attendants, 38 specially chosen and armed[31] noncommissioned officers were deployed.

As the liner *Schleswig-Holstein* delivered the first shot on the *Westerplatte* on September 1, 1939, at 0447 hours, and with it started the Second World War, the battle for the post office also began. For the support of the members of the *SS-Wachsturmbann* E[32] and the occupation of the *2. Polizei-Revier* in Danzig under the leadership of *Hauptmann der Schutzpolizei* Tornbaum, a section of the *III. Zug* of the *13. (I.G.) Kompanie* of the *SS-Heimwehr Danzig* also participated in the battles.

A *coup de main* like seizure of the postal building failed—20 meters in front of the office the German units remained in well managed resistance fire. In order to prevent military and civilian losses, the attack was initially stopped, and finally, at 1700 hours, with the aid of a howitzer of the Brigade Eberhardt, the building was weakened in preparation for an attack. In addition, firefighters succeeded in pumping gasoline into the basement rooms and igniting it, so that the Poles had to pull back from this position. At 1830 hours the Polish defenders surrendered. Anton Winter recounts the battle:

"I experienced the outbreak of the war on September 1, 1939, as a member of the III. Zug *der Infanteriegeschütz-Kompanie by the* SB-Heimwehr *Danzig. Our quarters were initially on the Bischofsberg above Danzig. The* 13. Kompanie *at this time consisted of three* Züge,

---

[31] The postal clerks had at their disposal over 30 army pistols. 1 revolver, 1 sack infantry munitions, 3 light machine guns, and 150 hand grenades.

[32] The *SS-Wachsturmbann E* was formed on July 3, 1939, by the order of *SS-Brigadeführer* Schäfer by decision of the Senate of the Free City of Danzig as police reinforcement of SS-men, and consisted of 4 *Hundertschaften* (groups of 100) and 1 *Kraftfahrstaffel. SS-Brigadeführer* Schäfter was appointed sole authorized person in police matters by the decree on June 28, 1939. The *SS-Brigadeführer* accomplished the formation of this police reinforcement with the authorization of the SS-*Oberabschnitt* Nordost because the Danzig police in number did not suffice, and were not to be called on for the numerous arising special assignments. The assignments of the *Sturmbann* were in July-September 1939 as follows:

1. Protection of the strategic operations in and around Danzig
2. Reinforcement of the *Revierpolizei*
3. Accompaniment of criminals from the Danzig prisons during transport from the sea route to Swinemünde
4. Protection of the city against a potential Polish attack. After the *SS-Heimwehr Danzig* was deployed in Dirschau by order of the *Wehrmacht*, the *SS-Wachsturmbann E* took over the tasks for which the *SS-Heimwehr* was originally designated.
5. The removal of Polish quarters in Danzig (Polish post office and railway administration, as well as participation in the battles for the Westerplatte). In doing so the *Sturmbann E* had 12 fallen and 20 wounded.

to each two light 4.5 cm infantry artillery—called Zigeunerartillerie. *The* Kompanieführer *was* SS-Hauptsturmführer *Schultz.* SS-Untersturmführer *Walter led the* III. Zug, *to which I belonged. The guns of the* I. *and* II. Zug *had rubber tires, and were therefore suitable for motorized mission. For lack of limber mot. the present Opel Blitz could only pull them. Our* III. Zug *had only iron* wheels, *also for drawing horses. But we did not have horses, so we had to move our guns in a* Mannschaftszug. *Later we loaded our guns on commandeered civilian vehicles. In our case it was the box wagon of a margarine factory.*

In addition to the light infantry artillery, we received two mortars from the First World War. The strength of the team remained the same, and because we were not trained on these heavy mortars, we later had considerable difficulties in action, and had to properly handle them. The caliber of this mortar was m. E. 15 cm.

Our Zug *was transferred before September 1, 1939, from Bischofsberg into the Danzig exhibition hall. From there we were on occasion ordered with our* Magarinegeschüt *to protect the Neufahrwasser port area. On August 31, 1939, the units of the* SS-Heimwehr Danzig *moved into their assembly areas. Only we, the* III. Zug (13. Kompanie) *remained for the time being in the exhibition hall, according to the order for the protection and a potential mission in the city.*

In the early morning hours of 1 September we were awakened by dull hums. The bombardment of the Westerplatte had begun. We eavesdropped until our Zugführer *came for us with the orders for duty. We then crawled to our guns in the box wagon and drove in front of the Polish post office, where we brought our guns in open fire position in the* Mannschaftszug. *The distance amounted to approximately 60 meters. Despite the heavy MG fire that we were met with, we shot grenade after grenade directly on and into the building. On the Kopfsteinpflasterstraße, without counter bearing, at each shot our gun sprang out of the platform, which complicated our shooting immensely. We had to tear open the plaster—in doing so our comrade Taynor fell from a shot in the head, and our* Zugführer *was badly injured on his arm.*

With the help of an armored reconnaissance vehicle of the Police a new attack on the post office was attempted, which, however, failed, and we again had losses. It was simply impossible to come over the strong wall and the iron railings and advance into the building. After our attack had failed, a break from battle arrived.

Also, the bombardment of a heavy howitzer of the Wehrmacht, *which was tracked in the meantime, the defenders could not be forced to the task. The Poles defended the post office with extraordinary bravery, and in belief that they would be relieved by the Polish cavalry who, as was well known, wanted to be in Berlin in seven days.*

Not until the late afternoon did it succeed under heavy covering fire to bring flammable material into the rooms and cellar, to ignite and thus smoke out the defenders. This caused them to give up, and we pulled our gun to the exhibition hall through a lining crowd.

During the evening our gun crew was ordered to report to the General der Polizei, *who wanted to, like he said, express his praise for our selfless mission against the Polish post office. The next day our gun was pulled to the* Kompanie *and deployed in battle for the Westerplatte.*"

The Poles, who after the Hague Land Warfare Convention did not have the status of combatants, were initially taken care of medically, and finally executed on October 5, 1939, as guerrillas.[33] Charlotte Kunthning experienced the beginning of the war as a nurse:

"My brother, Herbert Grätsch, was born in Danzig on August 1, 1922. When the first recruiters for the Heimwehr *in Danzig became active—my recollection is that all of them came from Munich—my brother was just 16 years old, and immediately reported. Apparently he was accepted right away, because on August 1, 1939, he had just turned 17, and on September 1, 1939, he had already been involved for several weeks. He participated in the battle for the Polish post office, and also in Oxhöft. There his friend Eduard Haubam stepped on a mine, and after pain lasting for hours he passed away. He went with me to a class in the school 'Schwarzes Meer.'*
I was a nurse in the Danzig municipal hospital, and had come to know everything from the other side. On the first day of war wounded transports came one after the other—a 20 year old had lain in the water at the Dirschau bridge for two hours. A gunshot wound through the cervical vertebrae—his entire body paralyzed. He lived for two more days. Landespolizei, Marineinfanterie, *Poles, and* Heimwehr, *everyone on this day. Whoever was injured, the worst was cared for first. Sometimes also a Pole. I shook whenever one came from the* Heimwehr. *It could have been my brother.*
Then, during the afternoon, the Poles from the Polish post office, burnt black, shaking with fear and pain. We wrapped their entire bodies in bandages with pain killing salve. They received injections of morphine, tetanus, and a gas gangrene serum. On the next day it was somewhat calmer. From our roof

---

[33]   In addition to the post office, in Danzig there were several other Polish quarters in which weapons were found. The *SS-Heimwehr* was not deployed in this operation. For the sake of completeness they should be named:

Location	What was secured:
Main Railway Station	1 machine gun
Polish TPO	1 machine gun, 4 rifles, 18 pistols, two crates of hand grenades
Polish Railway Administration	45 pistols
Polish Customs Inspection	15 rifles
Diplomatic Mission	1 machine gun, 5 rifles, 4 pistols
Polish Pfadfinderheim	1 machine gun
Polish Apartment Block Neufahrwasser	several rifles
Polish dormitory Langfuhr	several rifles
Polish Gymnasium	several rifles

I was able to see the dive-bomber attack on the Westerplatte. When the Poles surrendered, they came to us, and sometimes were already injured on the first day. When I loosened the head bandages of a young officer nearly half his face met mine."

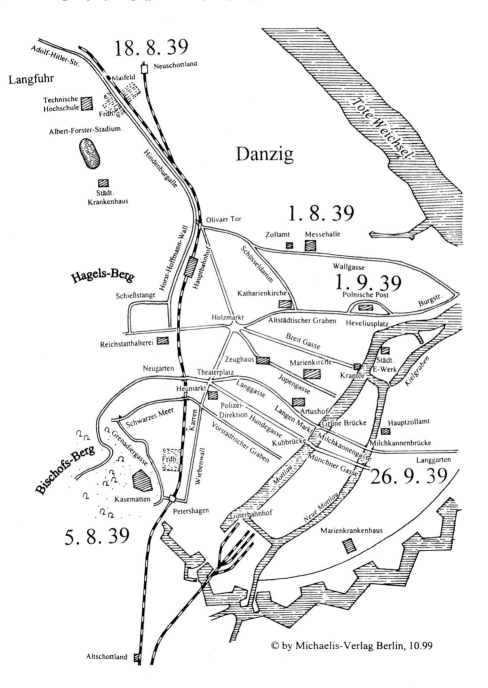

Nordbayerische Zeitung

Fürther Zeitung
Gegründet 1862

Fürther Volkszeitung
Gegründet 1885

Nr. 202   Fürth, den 30. August 1939   Mittwoch

Panzervorstoß gegen Danzig geplant

Schwere Ausschreitungen in Dirschau gegen Volksdeutsche

Der Führer machte den Vorschlag

einer deutsch-englischen Dauerregelung

Chamberlain im Unterhaus über die Antwort des Führers

Henderson beim Führer

London beginnt mit der Evakuierung

Polen unterbricht Danzigs Eisenbahnverkehr

Polnische Munitionskisten als »Lebensmittel« deklariert

Unser Recht steht fest

The evening before the war.

Nordbayerische Zeitung

Fürther Zeitung — Gegründet 1882

Fürther Volkszeitung — Gegründet 1885

Nr. 204   Fürth, den 1. September 1939   Freitag

Danzig ist heimgekehrt!

Aufruf Forsters an die Danziger Bevölkerung

Von jetzt ab Gewalt gegen Gewalt

Aufruf des Führers an die Wehrmacht

„Der polnische Staat hat die von mir erstrebte friedliche Regelung nachbarlicher Beziehungen verweigert …"

Telegramm an den Führer

Das neue Staatsgrundgesetz

Verbot des gesamten Luftverkehrs über dem deutschen Reichsgebiet

Zur Regelung des Danzig-Korridor-Problems

Deutschlands Vorschlag wurde abgelehnt

Zwei Tage vergebliches Warten auf einen bevollmächtigten polnischen Unterhändler

The first day of war.

Herbert Grätsch was deployed in front of the post office.

Damage by artillery on the anterior front.

Cutting from a newspaper on the battles for the Polish post office.

Das polnische Postamt in Danzig nach dem Kampf

Die Polen hatten das polnische Postamt in der „Freien Stadt" zu einer wahren Festung ausgebaut. Vom Dach und aus den Fenstern wurde von den polnischen Freischärlern auf die deutsche Bevölkerung und auf die deutschen Soldaten geschossen. Unsere Wehrmacht bereitete ihrem Treiben ein Ende

Aufnahme: PK. (Presse-Hoffmann)

Attack on the Polish post office

The Capture of Westerplatte

The Westerplatte is a low, sandy, and mostly forested peninsula with a length of 2 kilometers, and a maximum width of approximately 600 meters. At the beginning of the 19th century Poland, with help from the French, fortified the Westerplatte for defense against the Russians. Shortly before the First World War Germany built a gun emplacement situated near the seaside that was included in Poland's newly created defense system.

Due to its fine sandy beaches on the sea, before the First World War the Westerplatte was a popular seaside and vacation resort for the citizens of Danzig. When the Westerplatte was provided to the Polish government as a storage area for war material by decision of the *Völkerbundrat* on March 14, 1924, the Danzig population was not permitted admission. Two German policemen who were lodged in a small protective house in front of the Westerplatte monitored this.

The Polish crew consisted initially of two *Offiziere*, 20 *Unteroffiziere*, and 66 *Mannschaftsdienstgrade*. Through a constant exchange of Polish civilian workers with soldiers, the fighting strength increased to 210 men by the end of the 30s.

The preparations for the seizure of the Westerplatte were incumbent on the German *Kriegsmarine*. From this, a *Stoßkompanie* for a land operation was formed by the *III. Marine-Artillerie-Abteilung* in Swinemünde, and was commanded by Schleswig-Holstein.[34] On August 25, 1939, at 1044 hours the ship arrived in Danzig with the sounds of a military band, and at 1700 hours received the order to prepare for the attack on the Westerplatte as of 2100 hours. At 2120 hours the order was revoked. Not until August 31, 1939, did a radio message arrive to the *Kapitän zur See Kleikamp* that the attack on Poland was to begin the next day at 0445 hours.

Around 2330 hours the *Stoßkompanie* left the ship, and moved into starting positions for the attack. At 0447 hours the artillery and machinegun fire of the Schleswig-Holstein on the Westerplatte began. After breaches in the brick wall were made as a result of this, the *Marineartilleristen* attacked at 0456 hours. As the Poles persistently defended and inflicted great losses on the German attackers, the first attack at 0622 hours ceased.

Due to this development, the remainder of the *III. Zug* (*13./SS-Heimwehr Danzig*) received the order to transfer from the exhibition hall to the Westerplatte, and to support the further attack.

---

[34] This *Kompanie* consisted of 4 *Offiziere* and 225 *Unteroffiziere* and *Mannschaften*. It was organized in:
2 *Schützen-Züge*
2 *MG-Züge*
1 *Pionier-Zug*
1 *Granatwerfer-Zug*
1 *Nachrichten-Zug*

At 0855 hours the second attempt began to conquer the small peninsula. The SS members lost the connection around 1040 hours and went back. After the injury of the *Marinekompanieführer* Henningsen this attack also ceased at 1235 hours.

On the German side, surprised by the combat strength and the number of Poles, on September 2, 1939, the *Sturzkampfbomber* were to weaken the Westerplatte with bombing. Because the German losses amounted to roughly 50% of the deployed soldiers, it was nevertheless planned—equally unsuccessfully—to smoke out the defenders on 6 September. For this purpose, two railway wagons filled with gasoline were brought to the Westerplatte and ignited in order to set the forest on fire. However, the fire went out after a short time.

On 7 September another attack was carried out. For this purpose, members of the *Schleswig-Holstein* and the *SS-Wachsturmbann* E reinforced the *Stoßkompanie*.

Without coming across considerable resistance this time the soldiers advanced, and around 0945 hours saw the first white flags. According to statements of the captured Poles, the bombardment of the liner, as well as the bombardment by the *Luftwaffe*, was so demoralizing that on September 2, 1939, thoughts of surrender existed. However, when the next attack was carried out several days later they had time to recover. The *Oberkommando* of the *Wehrmacht* announced on Friday, September 8, 1939:

"The operations in Poland assumed the nature of a pursuit yesterday in many locations; only in single locations did it come to more serious battles.......
the occupation of the Westerplatte in Danzig ensued, their resistance was broken by Pioniere, Marinesturmkompanien, *and* SS-Heimwehr assisted by the Schleswig-Holstein...."

Günter Deinert experienced the battle for the Westerplatte as a 13-year-old:

"It was Friday, August 25, 1939, during the early morning when the liner Schleswig-Holstein *arrived in the Danzig-Neufahrwasser port. The warship came to a visit of goodwill, and moored near us at the wharf—across from the Westerplatte.*
From our house on the Olivaer Straße to the berth of the ship it was approximately 200 meters; in between there was only our yard, the old customs house on the Salzstraße, and an old Salzspeicher (salt storage unit) *from the time of Frederick the Great.*
A large crowd at the port greeted the ship. Also, for us children it was naturally an experience to see such a great warship up close. We spent every free hour near the ship. We were even permitted to visit the ship, and were given cap tallys, sleeve badges, and cigarette picture checks from the sailors.
The days passed, and September 1, 1939, came. It was very early in the morning when my father woke us. Something was not right. He went with us to the window and pointed at the street. Soldiers crept along the houses. What did that mean? We opened the parlor window,

and now clearly saw the soldiers with their weapons. Because I was too cold, I left the wing of the double window that opened inwards open a crack. A while later there was a terrible bang, and the casements hit me in the face. What had happened? As later became apparent, it was the first shot of the Schleswig-Holstein *on the Westerplatte. The vessel must have been hauled during the night to the Weichselmünde fort, and began from there with the bombardment of the Westerplatte.*

We quickly got dressed and went into the basement. Here we met already several occupants; nervousness prevailed. The shooting became stronger and stronger. My father had learned on the street that the war with Poland had begun, and that we again belonged to the German Reich. Extra newspapers were already passed around.

For safety reasons we were not permitted to leave the basement. One assumed that on the Westerplatte large amounts of munitions would be stored, and during an explosion the danger for Neufahrwasser would be massive. On the same day we were evacuated. My parents packed only a few emergency items together, and we moved to my grandparents' in Reichskolonie. However, here it was too crowded, and we drove to relatives in Oliva, who there had their own home. Oliva is more than eight kilometers away from the Westerplatte.

From the Volksempfänger, *and also the newspaper we learned of the war events, and also from the return home of Danzig into the Reich. Almost daily we risked getting close to Neufahrwasser. Because of this I was able to witness the* Stuka *attack on the Westerplatte from Paul-Beneke-Weg. Every day my father was in Neufahrwasser. He had also seen from the floor window of our house how on 7 September Polish soldiers displayed the white flag as a sign of surrender from a bunker.*

After the surrender of the Westerplatte became common knowledge, the evacuated occupants from Neufahrwasser returned. It looked awful in our apartment. All window panes on the yard side were in pieces, andd shards of glass were everywhere in the apartment. Kitchenware had fallen out of the cabinet and broken, while the preserving jars in the pantry had fallen from the shelves. We saw shots in our cooking stove that definitely came from rifle or machine gun bullets of the Polish soldiers.

I made my way to the harbor canal to get closer to the Westerplatte. On the way there I saw immense devastation on the Salzstraße. On the street were several bomb craters that came from the bombs of the Stukas. *The old customs house, which was only a few meters next to the bombsite, and also originated from the time of Frederick the Great, received heavy damage due to the vibrations.*

On the harbor canal on the Hafenstraße, a crane in front of the anchor storage shed had crashed on a railway wagon, and an ambulance of the Wehrmacht *from being bombarded. On the Weichselstraße and Schleusenstraße there were also several damaged homes that were in the line of fire of the* Schleswig-Holstein.

The Westerplatte itself looked desolate; the forest had suffered heavily under the bombardment, and many trees were crushed. The red wall that surrounded the Westerplatte on the landside was for the most part destroyed, and the area on the Westerplatte so empty, that one could even see a large bunker from Neufahrwasser.

Before Adolf Hitler visited Danzig on September 19, 1939, we could visit the Westerplatte. The forest had thinned out so much that one had an extensive field of vision. Behind the railroad gate was still the burned out tank wagon, with which one wanted to smoke out the Polish occupation.

We went further, and saw that a concrete bunker had received a direct bomb hit, and had collapsed and buried the Polish occupants. The old bunker, probably from the beginning of the 19th century, survived the attack. In the over one meter long strong soil of the bunker, bomb craters could be seen. Also, the barracks area was for the most part destroyed, the Westerplatte a single expanse of ruins."

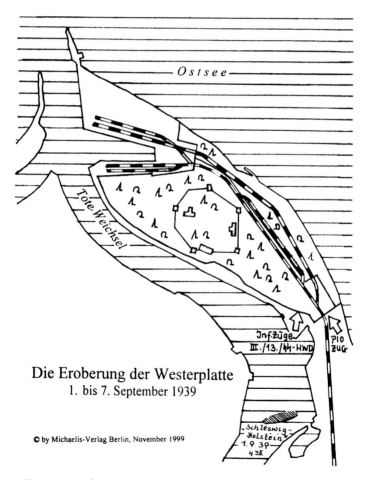

Die Eroberung der Westerplatte
1. bis 7. September 1939

The capture of the Westerplatte
September 1 to 7, 1939

Kriegsmarine wird eingesetzt

Westerplatte „kleines Verdun" — Kampf der „Schleswig-Holstein"

Von Kapitänleutnant **Werner Trendtel**

Der während des A
polnische Staat hat
Meere, der ihm volks
Weise zustand, erst dur
tat erzwungen. Ein s
falls nach Ansicht der
möglich auf Kosten de
Westpreußen.

So entstand für das
größerte Polen eine S
Länge, die dem dama
nischen Staatswesen e
gung und Anregunger
biet zu geben schien.

Das zu dieser Zeit
machte Deutsche Reich
enteignung tatenlos zu
Heine unbedeutende 9

stets auch)
en, wenn
t hatten,
hutz Dan=
sein sollte
he zu be=

ajaßes der
sinsaß des
Auslands=
„Schles=
n Danzig
sem Schiff
unserer
Artillerie

Training ship *Schleswig-Holstein* in the port of Danzig.

The shot *Unteroffizier mess.*

Destroyed bunker.

Visit by SS men.

Shelter.

Photographs of the Westerplatte after the end of the battles

Kampf um die Westerplatte

Die polnische Besatzung wird abgeführt

Stolz weht die deutsche Kriegsflagge über der eroberten Westerplatte

Das riesige Munitionslager brennt

Aufnahmen: PK.-Haine (Presse-Bild-Zentrale) (3). PK.-Lulinski (Atlantic) (1)

22

Aus der Kaserne wurde eine weiße Fahne als Zeichen der Kapitulation gehißt

From a newspaper

The Taking of Dirschau

The importance of Dirschau for the German leadership was the 837-meter long double bridge (railway and street) over the Vistula, which depicted the decisive connection between East Prussia and the German Reich. In the military-geographic description of Poland published by OKW in 1939, this bridge was listed as a highly important point.

Because one assumed that Poland was aware of its strategic importance, the safeguarding of the element of surprise would have been in the foreground of attack operations. Access was to be made from East Prussia, whereby the *SS-Heimwehr Danzig* ultimately had to intervene. In East Prussia, the *Gruppe* Medem[35] was formed of:

1 *Batallion* of the *Grenzwacht-Regiment 1*
1 *Infanterie-Ersatz-Batallion*
1 light *Artillerie-Abteilung*
1 *Kompanie* of the *Pionier-Batallion*
1 *Eisenbahn-Panzerzug*

The plan was designed such that sections of the *Gruppe* Medem were to occupy the bridge concealed in a freight train, while the *Luftwaffe* was to attack strategic points in Dirschau, and the *SS-Heimwehr* from the northwest had to make a connection to the bridge. Behind the freight train, which resembled a Trojan horse, the *Panzerzug* rode in order to secure the conquered bridge.

However, Polish railway officials at the Simonsdorf train station succeeded in redirecting the following *Panzerzug* and firing off a rocket flare. This flare alerted the Polish occupying troops at the bridge. When the freight train came to ride along the brid access was blocked. With the deployment of German air attacks, the Poles opened fire on the freight train and blew up the double bridge. The operation had therefore failed.

The *SS-Heimwehr Danzig* reached its initial positions on September 1, 1939, at around 0200 hours in the morning with the strength of approximately 1,200 men at Rambeltsch (to the north of Dirschau). The order read: take up and secure connection with the units from East Prussia. Herbert Schönfeld remembers:

"As of mid-August 1939 there were several false alarms. The kits for marching and attacking were always ready in the quarters. The alarms were sounded everywhere. No matter where

---

[35]   Gerhard Medem was born on October 14, 1893, in Zoppot. He entered military service on April 1, 1912, as *Fahnenjunker*. On November 20, 1913, he became *Leutnant* in the *Pionier-Batallion*. After his times in the *Reichswehr* Medem received as *Oberstleutnant* on October 1, 1937, the appointment to *Kommandeur der Pioniere* in the *WK I*. Promoted to *Oberst* on February 1, 1939, he formed the *Pionier-Regimentsstab z. b. V. 541* on August 19, 1939, as a training unit for the occupation of the Dirschau Vistula bridge. As of October 4, 1939, he commanded the *Pionierschule II*, and received the promotion to *Generalmajor* on September 1, 1941. In the official position of a *General der Pioniere* in the *Heeresgruppe Nord* on April 1, 1943, the appointment to *Generalleutnant* followed on September 1, 1943. Finally, he worked as *General der Pioniere* in the *Heeresgruppe* Kurland. Honored with the German Cross in silver, Medem died in 1953 in Soviet war captivity.

we were, in the cinema, in the theater, in pubs: Heimwehr Danzig *immediately to their quarters. Each vehicle, each taxi stopped to bring us to Matzkau as quickly as possible. During the night of September 1, 1939, our mission became reality. We had reported, and our* Kompaniechef *held a short speech: Over graves to new glory and to new deeds! Over Danzig-Ohra to the border towards Dirschau. Everything was uneasy at the beginning. We were even shot at once by our own flyers...."*

Around morning the soldiers crossed the border and marched into Damerau over Mühlbanz. At a railway embankment roughly 1,5000 meters from Dirschau's city border, there was heavy Polish resistance fire, whereby the units of the *SS-Heimwehr Danzig* were still in their positions until the evening. Not until after the support from the air force and heavy artillery could the men in Dirschau advance. In the city itself there was still isolated resistance that could not ultimately be broken until September 5, 1939. Wenzel Woldrich reported on the gravity of the mission:

"I was Rifleman I manning a light machine gun, and was already wounded on the first day of battle. Ours, the first Kompanie, *whose* I. Zug *I belonged to, suffered the most attacks on this day. In our* Zug *alone there were five dead and five wounded...."*

Willi Fischer was also wounded on September 1, 1939:

"I was born in Danzig on May 29, 1917. After attending the Volksschule *I went to the* Realschule *in Marienburg, and was from 1936 to 1938 a recruit in the* Reiter-Regiment I *in Insterburg. Because I assumed our home was threatened by Polish invasion, I and quite a number of other reservists went to the* Heimwehr. *We were picked up in Tiegendorf, and finally arrived in Berlin-Adlershof. I was badly wounded on the first day by Rambeltsch Rückmarkschuß. Off to the Danzig hospital, then on an airplane to Berlin-Hohenlychen. Operation—a silver plate was inserted, and then back to Danzig. In the hospital,* SS-Obersturmbannführer *Goetze in the presence of* SS-Hauptsturmführer *Baier presented me the Iron Cross II. Afterwards I went to the Bayrisch-Zell military hospital."*

Ernst Päpper remembers:

"On the morning of September 1, 1939, I was likewise stationed at the railway embankment in front of Dirschau with my Gruppe. *Because the order to proceed only to the railway embankment did not reach me, with my men I advanced over the embankment into close proximity to a community garden area, left of the underpass. Rifleman Behrend was wounded. When I determined that there could be no advancement here due to the heavy enemy fire, I went back with my entire* Gruppe *behind the railway embankment. Nearly the entire* Batallion *was still in their initial positions there. The Poles defended themselves bravely once more."*

When the air attacks ended, and the defense of the city borders could be wrestled down, the *SS-Heimwehr Danzig* advanced to the by now destroyed Vistula bridge, and together with detachments from the *Gruppe* Medern secured the establishment of a pontoon bridge from the east to the west over the Vistula. Leo Wilm remembers the first days of September:

"As a motorcycle despatch rider, I was directly under Kommandeur SS-Obersturmbannführer *Hans-Friedemann Goetze. On August 31, 1939, he gave me the assignment to ride to Rambeltsch, and set up his command post at a farm. He wanted to follow later at 2 o'clock in the morning with the* Batallion. *On the way there I saw* Langrohr *guns by Praust. My thoughts were: Will it become serious this time? In Rambeltsch I immediately searched for the farmer, who was already informed. I did not need to explain the particulars to him. At 2 in the morning the* Kommandeur *also arrived, gave me a record of where the single* Kompanien *were located, and ordered me to get the* Kompaniechef *for the issuing of orders. He explained the situation, and said that at 0445 hours a double decker would come and launch a red flare—that would be the signal for the beginning of our attack.*
During the attack we came to a railway embankment where there was no further advance. After an in-depth observation, the Kommandeur den Adjutanten *Westermann ordered me to fetch a* Zugführer *with anti-tank guns as well as hand grenades, in order to undertake a* Stoßtrupp *to Dirschau under his command. Despite heavy enemy fire we succeeded in coming through the underpass and taking cover in the roadside ditches towards Dirschau. The anti-tank gun followed us, but fell out after a short period. Nevertheless, we neared the first houses and took care of single MG nests; however, we pulled back again. After our return Goetze received a radio message that aircraft were deployed for support in order to ease the taking of Dirschau.*
It must have been approximately 1500 hours when the skies opened the floodgates, because a thunderstorm and heavy rain poured down on us. One could no longer tell the difference between the thunder and firings from guns. When the flyers came and dropped their bombs over Dirschau our positions were also hit, and we had losses. This occurred because our men had gotten rid of their wet tunics after the rain, and because of our brown shirts we looked like Polish soldiers."

The *Zug* of Kurt Enss was initially deployed in Danzig for safeguarding. Not until later did the remainder of the *SS-Heimwehr Danzig* follow:

"While we were stationed here on the Luzernefeld and waited for the enemy attack, other Kompanien *of the* SS-Heimwehr *had the assignment of taking Dirschau.*
SS-Oberscharführer *Krone and a radio operator remained in constant radio contact with them, so everyone knew what was happening on the battlefield. We learned of the losses from 'grenade throwers' and the feared sharpshooters, whose motorcycle despatch rider in particular fell victim. They lay in wait in the trees for their victims: it was mostly aimed headshots, which meant certain death.*

At our location nothing took place on this day. During the late evening fatigue overwhelmed me, and I fell asleep until we received the order to assemble. We pulled out and rode to Dirschau. Our SS-Obersturmführer *Prechtl went to each vehicle and cheered us up with his winsome smile, which was welcome to us in this moment, because he always had a joking comment.*

When we arrived in Dirschau at the break of day, the IG-Kompanie *and the* Panzerabwehr-Kompanien *were already there, war beaten, and the* Schützen-Kompanien *considerably dirtied with mud. Our* Batallionskommandeur *Goetze was also here. The city was taken on the first day by the* SS-Heimwehr. *At the time purges were underway in several quarters. Around midday we marched towards new assignments, and established a secure position outside of the city at an altitude with a wide view. Apparently, there were suspicions that the Poles wanted to re-conquer Dirschau, as it was still unclear where the Polish units were staying.*

The next day the positions were abandoned again. When we took our seats on the personnel carrier, we received the order that the entire Batallion should *first ride through Danzig on the return journey, and afterwards to Matzkau for an overnight stay. When we drove into the completely darkened city, an indescribable thunderous jubilation wwwas received from all sides. We were showered with flowers and candy. It was astounding where the thousands of people got everything from on this Sunday, when all the shops had closed...."*

Die Einnahme von Dirschau
1. bis 5. September 1939

© by Michaelis-Verlag Berlin, November 1999

Freistaat Danzig
Hohenstein
SS-Heimwehr
Rambeltsch
Mühlbanz
Damerau
Ostpreußen
Gruppe Medem
Simonsdorf
Weichsel
Polen
Dirschau
Marienburg

The Taking of Dirschau
September 1 to September 5, 1939

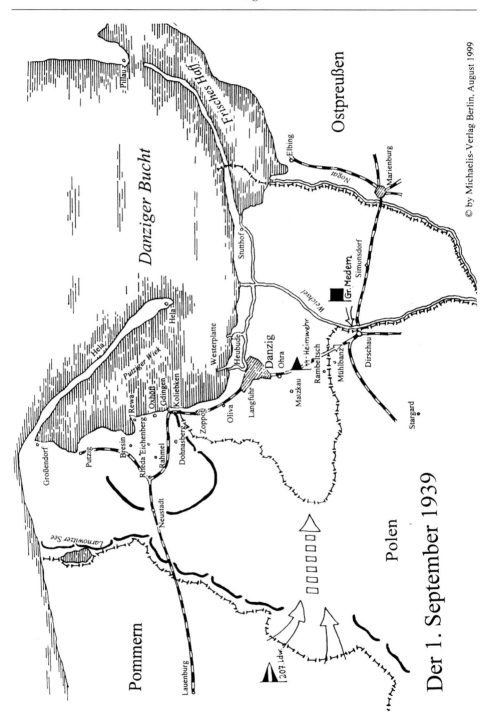

In the small town of
Rambeltsch.

March-off.

Advance on Dirschau.

Preparation in front of the Polish border

Throwers at entrenchment in front of Dirschau.

View in the direction of Dirschau.

The Vistula Bridge detonated by the Poles.

Dirschau and the destroyed Vistula Bridge

The Storming of Oxhöfter Kämpe

On September 1, 1939, the *207. Infanterie-Division*[36] from the Bütow area was dispatched in the direction of Berent, in order to break through Danzig and separate the area in a north and south corridor. On the evening of the same day the first detachments of the Division reached the border of the Free State of Danzig by Ochsenkopf.

The following day the connection of the *Landwehr-Division* with the Brigade Eberhardt was established, which was located east of Zuckau. The *Landwehr-Infanterie-Regiment* 374 under the command of the Brigade was ordered to halt the 12-kilometer wide front sector of Quaschin-Steinkrug against Polish breach attempts in the south. On 7 September the Danzig powers held the line Koliecken - Forest southwest of Gr. Katz - Dohnasberg - Kölln - Steinkrug.

The *SS-Heimwehr* was previously ordered back to Danzig-Zoppot and, boisterously greeted by the population, placed there under the Brigade Eberhardt. Detachments also came into the area of command of the *207. Infanterie-Division* in Neustadt. On September 10, 1939, on the one hand the conquered areas of remaining Polish units were purged, while on the other hand began to reconnoiter the Oxhöfter Kämpe for the imminent attack. Leo Wilm reported on this day:

"With a day of rest in Danzig, it was then in the direction of Zoppot, and here we entered a new stage. Nothing happened here for two days; nevertheless, I was unable to rest. Because I had a B-Krad as a motorcycle despatch rider, everyone wanted to ride with me. No matter if it was to the Kompanien *or a command post, I was always underway. One evening I laid down next to my motorcycle, exhausted and worn out, and wanted to rest some. When I heard my name called, I acted deaf. Suddenly someone shook me and said 'Wilm, get up, we have to drive on.' Because I thought some lazy guy had discovered me and wanted to ride somewhere, I blurted out the saying from Götz von Berlichingen. The answer was 'I know, but I'm not doing it.'—The voice of our* Adjutant, SS-Obersturmführer *Westermann. I was completely shocked, but he gave a dismissive gesture, said that it was ok, and that I should get my motorcycle ready. The journey continued to* Landespolizei *headquarters. After the return Westermann said to me that we would drive through a* Stoßtrupp *the next day. I took part in this operation with my motorcycle, along with* SS-Obersturmführer *Westermann and* SS-Hauptsturmführer *Baier with two men in a military utility vehicle.*

---

[36]   The *207. Infanterie-Division* was formed on August 26, 1939, and *Division 3. Welle* in the *Wehrkreis II* Pommern through the *Landwehrkommandeur* Stargard. It consisted of the *Infanterie-Regimenter 322, 368*, and 374, as well as the *Artillerie-Regiment 207*, and the further *Divisionseinheiten 207*.

It must be stated here that SS-Obersturmbannführer *Goetze had an accident with his military utility vehicle, and* SS-Hauptsturmführer *Baier led the* Batallion.[37] *After approximately 15 km we encountered resistance, but the enemy pulled back, and we were able to advance. We saw a gruesomely bloody deed here: a man was crucified to a barn door, and a family of seven killed in their home and nailed to the table with their tongues. The crucified man was a forester of German descent, and the family likewise of German descent. The villagers who did not flee with the Polish soldiers explained this to us. A report of this crime was given to the* Kommandeur *of the* Landespolizei....*
Another time I was underway again with my motorcycle. In the sidecar I had previously dropped off SS-Unterscharführer *Michaelis at a* Kompanie. *On the way back I drove through a forest, and suddenly people from the* Landespolizei *stopped me, and forced me to keep my hands up. I was completely shocked when I saw the rifles aimed at me. They asked who I was, from where I was coming, and other things. Because many of their comrades had already been attacked and murdered in this forest by the Poles, they could not believe at all that I had driven through so effortlessly.... They themselves no longer dared to go into the forest.*
From the Brigade Eberhardt headquarters, where we reported, I drove from Danzig back to the unit again. On this trip I visited my parents without a large detour, because from Danzig to Zoppot I always had to drive by our home. I first met my father. My mother was underway with our neighbor, Frau Heidemann. It was not long before they came back. When the neighbor saw me, she fainted. When she came around again, she explained to us that she had gone on a walk with my mother to explain to her that I had fallen in Dirschau. However, she did not have the heart, and hoped that the party would tell my parents. I asked her what gave her the idea that I had fallen? An acquaintance had all the names of those fallen in Dirschau. Thank God I was not dead...."

On September 11, 1939, the enemy was thrown out of Lensitz by the *Gruppe* Eberhardt and from Rahmel by the *207. Infanterie-Division*. Altogether roughly 300 prisoners were taken. The preparation for the attack on the Oxhöfter Kämpe had begun.
The target of the Brigade Eberhardt was Gdingen, which a few years prior was a small outlying fishing village with a few straw covered houses. Not until the end of the 20s was a large port built by Poland which, together with the Oxhöfter port, developed into a war and trade port.

---

[37]   After *SS-Obersturmbannführer* Goetze had a car accident on September 2, 1939, and thereby suffered a concussion and a metatarsal fracture, *SS-Hauptsturmführer* Baier initially led the *SS-Heimwehr*. *Oberstleutnant* Graf von Rittberg later took over the reinforced *Batallion*.

On 12 September the Danzig troops advanced to Straße Bahnhof Kielau - Sagorsch with their focus on Lensitz, and in advancing reached the line Kl. Katz - Krückwald - Grünhof. The following resulted in the breakthrough to Straße Ciessau - Sagorsch, and the new line Steinberg - Grabau - Kielau directly in front of Gdingen. Because the Polish soldiers pulled back to Oxhöft, Gdingen was able to be occupied without struggle on September 14, 1939. Georg Diehl remembers:

"Our Zug *was assigned to the* Polizeikompanie Thiele. *Without any significant events we reached the street of Gdingen towards Warsaw before the trigonometrical point on the Dohnarsberg. On the hill ground fortifications could be recognized, and the Poles repulsed a* Spähtrupp. *A gun was placed for securing the street in the direction of Gdingen, while two remained on standby. Each day a time was established for the attack, and again delayed, because this or that* Batterie *was still not in position. After the second day we were relieved by the* III. Zug. *For us it was not an enjoyable occasion, because each would like to have been a part of the spectacle. When the* Zug *came for relief, the* SS-Oberscharführer *asked our* Kompanieführer *for a motorcycle despatch rider because his had fallen out due to an accident; in other words, I was permitted to stay.*

The next morning, after artillery preparations, the attack was to begin. The SS-Oberscharführer *remained with two* guns *on the street to Gdingen, and the third* gun *had to go around the hill. I drove approximately 100 meters ahead, as I was to reconnoiter the path.*

It had come thus far. First heavy grenades from the railroad guns roared over our heads, then 21 cm and 15 cm grenades, followed by 10.5 cm and 4.5 cm grenades. The attack began. We drove as fast as the path allowed, and could see several Poles disappear. They also shot bac—but without success.

I moved on in order to make my own impression, and was finally the first who stood on the Dohnarsberg. The collaboration with the Polizei *was good. At the daily delivery of the report of the situation of our Zug on the* Batallion*command post in an inn I got to know the* Kommandeur. *He was the only one from his* Stab *who did not sleep and, as he said to me, also the only active one of his* Batallion. *When he then heard that I came from Upper Bavaria (he was from Munich) I had gained his trust.*

Although he had a Kradmeldestaffel, *I had to bring daily reports to him nearly every night to the* Brigade. *Citizens of Danzig always stood in front of the* Brigade *command post, and wanted to be informed of the newest situation. After a short report they stuffed my coat with so much candy and tobacco products that I could hardly move. My comrades from the* Zug *were always excited about the nightly rides. With this* PolizeiBatallion*we then arrived at the port of Gdingen.*

Everything was quiet and peaceful. Suddenly, approximately 50 meters in front of us an old Maxim-MG chugged. Without hitting our Opel Blitz, the Poles simply shot into the house wall. After this surprise, three comrades pulled both frightened riflemen from their hideaway. These were the last Polish greetings to us here.

Our Zug *then moved to abandoned foreign quarters on the hill across from Hela. From here, like in a movie theater, we could observe the bombardment of the peninsula by the* Schleswig-Holstein *and the* Schlesien....*"*

While the *Danziger Gruppe* proceeded towards the Oxhöfter Kämpe[38] from the south, the *207. Infanterie-Division* attacked from the west and north. In the north, the *Grenzwacht-Regiment 42* (Wuth) secured the Hela peninsula, and purged the area north of the Rheda from the enemy. The *Grenzwacht-Regiment 32* (von Bothmer), with subordinate detachments of the *SS-Heimwehr Danzig* under the command of Graf von Rittberg, proceeded from the north towards Oxhöfter Kämpe. With the support of *Sturzkampfbomber* and artillery, the *Landwehr-Regiment 368* attacked the Kämpe on the western border.

Above all, the village of Kasimier and the Eichenberg (66.4 meter altitude) had to be taken as primary Polish strongholds. While the attack on Kasimir slowly progressed, Polish units approached Rahmel in a counterattack. Through heavy battles the German troops were able to fight off the attack. During these battles, *SS-Untersturmführer* Peiper (*1./SS-Heimwehr Danzig*), deployed there with his *Zug*, received the Iron Cross 2nd Class for the combat with a Polish *Panzerzug*.

The Eichenberg was taken by storm on September 12, 1939, by units of the *SS-Heimwehr Danzig*. Only a cobblestone street led through the miry meadow terrain that was, in addition, put under water by several brooks built by the Poles. The attempt to occupy the Eichenberg in a sudden and unexpected operation failed. Leo Wilm remembers:

"Our unit was transferred, and came to the battle for the Oxhöfter Kämpe by Eichenberg. This was strongly fortified by the Poles, and left our attack paralyzed in front of the river. From the location of Bresin, I had to make an exploratory trip forward with Adjutant *Westermann. Because only one street led in the direction of Eichenberg, it was easily accessible to the Poles, and was constantly under fire. As the bullets breezed by our ears, I automatically stopped. The* Adjutant *tapped on my shoulder and said, 'Wilm, not every bullet hits.'*

---

[38]   North of the Dginger port, a mountain ridge stretches into the Gulf of Danzig that is weakly forested: die Oxhöfter Kämpe. It is comprised of a high plateau whose highest elevation is the Eichenberg. Poland had provided this area with numerous positions because it offered good possibilities for defense. There were concrete bunkers, barbed wire, trenches, and gunners' stations of all kinds, as well as machine gun nests and artillery positions favorably fitted into the terrain. In the east the Oxhöfter Kämpe was bordered by the Gulf of Danzig, while in the south it was covered by war facilities and trade ports of Gdingen and Oxhöft built in 1926. In the north and west there were broad areas of swamplands. It was a disadvantage for the Poles that there was no forest through to the west border of the Kämpe, so that they were exposed without any defense to the attacking German *Sturzkampfbomber*.

I continued to drive, and we did not come much further, because approximately 20 meters in front of the river the fire was so strong that we were again forced to stop and look to the trenches for cover. The Adjutant *was shot in the head and was immediately killed. My motorcycle was shot. I had to remain under cover until it was dark, and then pulled back."*

Ernst Päpper was wounded during the battles:

"While our unit had few losses in Dirschau, the battles for the Oxhöfter Kämpe on 10 and 12 September were difficult and costly. On the evening of September 10, 1939, I was deployed with my Gruppe *as a strong* Spähtrupp *at the Kämpe, and lost four of my men to mines and a close shot of one of our own guns, which stood in firing position on a slope in our initial positions at Bresin. September 12 was a dark day for me, as I was shot in the head...."*

On 13 September, in the Eichenberg area, there were heavy Polish counterattacks. By restricting the encircled area, however, the opposition's room for operation constantly decreased. Himmler mentioned the storming of Eichenberg by the *SS-Heimwehr Danzig* on September 12, 1939, at the Gauleiter meeting on August 3, 1944:

"I want to randomly mention several examples that I as Reichsführer-SS *and* Führer *of the* Waffen-SS *experienced throughout distressing years— that I can calmly say today—day by day and month by month. In 1939, for example, the Oxhöfter Kämpe at Danzig was stormed. The* Batallion*that took it by storm is a* Batallion*of the* SS-Heimwehr Danzig. *We were unfortunate that the* Regimentskommandeur *was wounded, or had met with an accident the previous day, and was therefore taken out of duty. From the famous Pommeranian* Landwehrdivision *that was then taken in reaction, Graf Rittberg was placed to this* Batallion*as* Batallionskommandeur. *The Oxhöfter Kämpe was then taken by storm with the* Batallion. *Then it was reported: the umpteenth Pomeranian* Landwehrdivision *stormed the Oxhöfter Kämpe with the Grafen Rittberg. That also appeared in the* Wehrmachtbericht.[39] *At the time I was in Zoppot, and said 'My* Führer, *that is not at all true, that was my* Batallion.' *Then the* Führer *said 'It was the* Batallion *Graf Rittberg; there is no such thing. I said 'My* Führer, *I can prove that, our dead are lying around, you only need to look.' Then it was questioned: yes, naturally it is a* Batallion*of the* SS, *but it was on this day under this and that Division's command, and the* Batallion*was naturally named after the* Kommandeur— *that was not at all necessary—and therefore it is called the* Batallion*Graf Rittberg."*

After the occupation of Gdingen, the German forces (*Korps Kaupisch*[40]) were reorganized and positioned at Oxhöft. This city was cited by the Poles as a stronghold,

---

[39]   The storming of the Oxhöfter Kämpe was not mentioned in the *Wehrmachtbericht*; here Himmler, as he often was, is mistaken.

[40]   Leonhard Kaupisch was born in Elberfeld on September 1, 1878. On March 18, 1898, he entered military service, and became *Leutnant* in the *Fußartillerie-Regiment 6* on August 18, 1899. After his time in the *Reichswehr*

and was built stronger than Gdingen. One day after the Red Army surprisingly crossed the Polish eastern border,[41] on 18 September the German troops in the Oxhöfter Kämpe proceeded to move on a major offensive. In the south, detachments of the *Brigade* Eberhardt from Gdingen encountered the *Kolonie* Oblusch, and held them during heavy counterattacks. During the battles they took approximately 1,000 prisoners—an even higher number of 1,700 prisoners made the troops of the *207. Infanterie-Division* deployed around Eichenberg. After partially despairing Polish resistance, the German troops conquered Oxhöft. On September 19, 1939, the Polish *Festungskommandant* presented the stronghold to the troops of the *Brigade* Eberhardt at 1730 hours. On the same day Hitler visited Danzig, and on September 20, 1939, Gdingen. Concerning this, *Generalmajor* Eberhardt ordered:

"9/19   0800 hours arrival of the Führerzug *in the Lauenburg region*
Subsequent journey in car, without stops over Neustadt, Schönwalde, Kölln, and Oliva to Zoppot. The named street is to be kept clear on 9/19 from 0800 hours to 1000 hours from vehicles of all kinds. Inspection as of Kölln by Feldgendarmerie *at the urging of the* Quartiermeisterabteilung.
The units on the street have the opportunity to greet the Führer *during his passage. Parade formation does by no means come into question. Flawless attire, German salutation. Address:* 'Mein Führer. '
No flowers may be thrown or presented.
Around 1200 hours the people rally on the Langen Markt.
Standortältester Danzig regulates the securing of a seat for military spectators.
Attire: field dress, cap, small decorative buckle, gray gloves.
Quartiermeisterabteilung *directly regulates the participation of smaller sections of the rear, and reports approximate number of participants until 9/18*
1400 hours at Standortältester *Danzig.*
9/20   0900 hours departure to Gdingen, Kommandant *Gdingen with* SS-Oberführer *Schäfter regulates cordon on the journey until and in Gdingen. Greeting of the* Führer *by the troops positioned in Gdingen according to given orders for 9/19 for the car journey.*

---

he was *Stabschef* of the *2. Division.* Assigned to *Generalmajor* (November 1, 1930) and *Artillerieführer V,* on September 30, 1932, he withdrew from active duty as *Generalleutnant* (March 1, 1932). On April 1, 1934, reentry into the *Luftwaffe* as *Kommandierender General* and Commander in the *Luftkreis 2* followed. Discharge followed on March 31, 1938. As of January 1, 1939, he stood at the disposal of the army as *General der Flieger.* After the beginning of the war he was initially *Kommandeur* of the *Grenzabschnittskommando I,* and then of the *Korps Kaupisch.* From October 15, 1939, to April 10, 1942, he commanded (as of September 1, 1940: *General der Artillerie*) the *XXXI. A. K.* At the same time he was *Militärbefehlshaber* of the German troops in Denmark from April 9 until May 31, 1940. On June 30, 1942, finally withdrawn from service, Kaupisch died on September 26, 1945, in Weimar.
[41]   Interestingly enough, the Western Allies did not declare war on the Soviet Union—even after the invasion into the English sphere of interest (Scandinavia) during the Soviet-Finish Winter war 1939/40!

Concluding journey through Gdingen. Formation of the following units:

1. *Sections of the* Grenz-Schutz-Abschnitt-Kommandos I
2. 1./Infanterie-Regiment 2
3. Aufklärungsschwandron *Neuß*
4. *From the* SS-Heimwehr, Kompanie Their, *including* Pak.-Zug *assigned to the* Kompanie *during the attack of the Oxhöfter Kämpe*
5. Marine-Stoßtrupp-Kompanie

Dress uniform: steel helmet, rifle at the feet, bayonet not fixed.
Führer *in front of the right wing. Detailed instructions to the leaders of the units named above takes place on 9/18, 1230 hours in Gdingen Rathaus.*
Heightened attention of all Truppen *at the enemy.*
The readiness for action of the troop may not be minimized by the visit of the Führer.
Conspicuous behavior of the enemy is to be reported immediately to the group command post."

In addition to detachments of the Navy and *SS-Heimwehr Danzig,* also two *Hunderschaften* (group of one hundred) of the *SS-Wachsturmbann E* were deployed during the *Führer's* visit for the securing of Zoppot, Oliva, and Danzig.[42]
On 21 September the troops marched to the north to move into position in the Großendorf area, countering the Polish occupation of Hela. They had at their command numerous concrete facilities and several artillery positions—above all on the eastern section of the peninsula to the open sea. The *SS-Heimwehr* did not witness the surrender of the last Polish units in this area on September 30, 1939, as well as the German victory parade in Warsaw on October 1, 1939, in the line of duty.

---

[42]   This *SS-Wachsturmbann E* (Eimann) guarded, as of October 1939, the Neufahrwasser prison camp. Stutthof and Grenzdorf, in which Poles were arrested who were to be deported to central Poland (*Generalgouvernement*). 2 *Hundertschaften* (groups of 100) were used for this reason until December 1939 to liquidate approximately 3,400 people referred to as incurable mental patients. Sections were also deployed at the request of the *Gestapo* to accompany the transport of Jews to Vienna and Preßburg. In January 1940 the *SS-Wachsturmbann E* was transferred as *II. Sturmbann* into the *15. SS-Totenkopf-Standarte.*

On the march.

The equipment is being brought in order.

In front of Dirschau.

Oxhöfter Kämpe

Transfer into the Oxhöfter Kämpe.

During the advance.

Minenwerfer "Iwan" at Eichberg.

Oxhöfter Kämpe

Short break from duty by
Neustadt.

Military utility vehicle
with MG bullet holes.

Rations supplies at
Oxhöfter Kämpe.

Over Neustadt to Oxhöfter Kämpe

Im Kahn die Hebamme geholt

Zwischen Geschützdonner — Brief einer Danzigerin

Eine Danzigerin, Besitzerin eines kleinen Anwesens bei einem der kleinen Weichselorte, schildert im folgenden einer Freundin die Kriegsereignisse, so wie sie sich für die Umwohner Danzigs, die mit fieberhafter Spannung das Geschehen verfolgten, darstellten.

B......., den 17. September 1939

Liebe L. Auf Deine Karte melde ich mich als lebendig zur Stelle. Mein Haus steht, und dicke Weintrauben reifen an seiner Südwand, schwere Birnen hängen an den Bäumchen bis fast zur Erde. — Ja, auf den Nerven ist arg getrommelt worden, und eben trommelt es wieder, nach zwei Tagen himmlischer Ruhe; wahrscheinlich beschießt die „Schleswig-Holstein" Hela.

Das war das Nervenzerrüttende hier: In der Stille hört man jeden Schuß, das Haus wankte, die Fenster klirrten, man sah jeden

Sturzbomber seine Last absetzen und hörte den Einschlag, man sah die Schiffe feuern, sah die Westerplatte brennen, sah jeden Heuschober, den die Polen auf der Danziger Höhe in Brand steckten. Bei Westwind hörte man sogar das Maschinengewehrfeuer, und als die Dirschauer Brücke in die Luft flog, schütterten bei uns die Fenster.

Wir alle hatten die Häuser bis unters Dach voll Flüchtlinge. Ich hatte nur eine Doktorfamilie mit vier Kindern aus Danzig und eine Bekannte aus Zoppot. Aber die anderen bekamen die Leute, die wegen der Westerplatte aus Neufahrwasser evakuiert wurden. Unser kleines B., das regulär 800 Einwohner zählt, hatte 3000 Flüchtlinge! Es war ein Leben hier wie im Zeltlager. In den Waschkesseln wurde für alle gekocht. Viel Bromberger waren hier, die tagelang um ihre

Ethnic German population is evacuated from the combat area of the corridor.

From the perspective of the civilian population

The men of the *SS-Heimwehr Danzig* await the order to attack.

At the mortar.

In the trenches.

Kompanie Urbanitz in the battles for Oxhöfter Kämpe

Initial positions for the storming of Eichenberg.

Anxiously waiting.

The marshland at Eichenberg.

Battle for Eichenberg

Members of the *IG-Kompanie* Schulz march in Gdingen without a struggle on September 14, 1939.

The *Standortkommandantur* in Gdingen (Gotenhafen).

Invasion in Gdingen

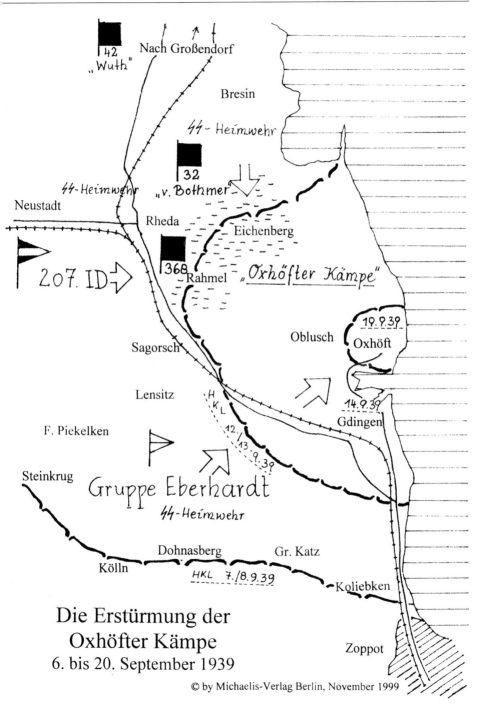

Die Erstürmung der
Oxhöfter Kämpe
6. bis 20. September 1939

© by Michaelis-Verlag Berlin, November 1999

The Storming of Oxhöfter Kämpe
September 6-20, 1039

March to Oxhöft.

Invasion in Oxhöft on September 19, 1939.

Bombardment of the Oxhöfter port area.

Mission Oxhöft

Hitler visits Danzig on September 19, 1939.

Continuation of the journey to Gdingen, now Gotenhafen, on September 20, 1939.

Hitler in Danzig and Gdingen

Map after the end of the battles against Poland.

Der Führer im Kampfgebiet von Oxhöft.

Zusammen mit Generalfeldmarschall Göring und Gauleiter Forster besichtigte der Führer das Kampfgebiet auf den Höhen von Oxhöft, wo der letzte hartnäckige Widerstand der Nordgruppe der polnischen Korridorarmee gebrochen wurde.

Poland's defeat

The Siege of Warsaw

After the capture of the Oxhöfter Kämpe, the Poland campaign had ended for the mass of the Brigade Eberhardt, including the *SS-Heimwehr Danzig*, and the *Landespolizei-Regiment II* received further orders for duty. The Regiment was to reinforce the German troops in a siege and potential attack on Warsaw. For this purpose, the Regiment had placed at its command 6 *Granatwerfer*, together with crew of the *Maschinengewehr-Kompanie* of the *SS-Heimwehr Danzig*.

Warsaw and Modlin were cited as strongholds from the political side, and until September 22, 1939, were entirely surrounded by German troops. After the evacuation of the diplomatic corps, as well as non-Polish citizens, the continuous air and artillery bombardment and *Granatwerfer* began. For the latter purpose, the *Granatwerfergruppen* of the *SS-Heimwehr Danzig* were also utilized. Infantry attacks on both strongholds, however, did not take place due to the expected heavy losses in the street and house battles.

On September 27, 1939, the church bells in the Warsaw stronghold sounded as a sign of surrender. For the members of the *SS-Heimwehr Danzig*, this meant a march back to Danzig, from which they were commanded to Dachau on 29 September.

The Disbandment of the *SS-Heimwehr Danzig*

On September 26, 1939, the *Gruppe* Eberhardt—and the *SS-Heimwehr Danzig*—left the *Korps Kaupisch* and returned to Danzig, celebrated by the population. The Danzig Vorposten reported:

"SS-Heimwehr *received jubilantly at their entrance*
Although announced only yesterday in the midday hours that the SS-Heimwehr Danzig *was returning, and the* Gauleiter *would greet them in front of the Artushof on the Langen Markt, around 1500 hours a vast crowd gathered on the Langen Markt in order to witness the return home of our* SS-Heimwehr Danzig....
Several minutes after 1500 hours the long motorcade neared the Langen Markt, coming from the Milchkannengasse. Calls of 'Heil' rang out, getting louder and louder, that did not end when the first car, in which the Kommandeur *of the* SS-Heimwehr Danzig, Obersturmbannführer *Goetze, sat, appeared under the* Grüner Tor. *The excited crowd broke through the cordons and pushed towards the motorcade, that only drudgingly could carve the way to the Artushof, where the Gauleiter of the* SS-Heimwehr *waited. In front of the Artushof,* Obersturmbannführer *Goetze stepped out of the car and made a report to the* Gauleiter.
Car after car rolled by, and in front the flag that the Gauleiter ceremoniously presented on 18 August on the Maifeld of the SS-Heimwehr Danzig. *It lasted nearly a half hour before the long motorcade reached its end. Still jubilant, the immense crowd pushed forward and offered the Gauleiter an endless heartfelt ovation at the conclusion.*
The SS-Heimwehr Danzig, *who participated in several military operations, such as the storming of Dirschau, the Westerplatte, and Oxhöft—to name only a few—moved back into the* SS-Heimwehr *Matzkau barracks yesterday afternoon, where they will find their deserved relaxation and recuperation for the next days."*

Der Völkische Beobachter wrote on September 27, 1939:

"Storm of excitement for the SS-Heimwehr Danzig
The SS-Heimwehr Danzig *has returned after difficult battles for the protection of Danzig. They outstandingly participated in the storming of Dirschau, the Westerplatte, and Oxhöft. Eight men of the* SS-Heimwehr Danzig *were honored with the Iron Cross by the* Führer...."

Three days later the transfer to southern Germany began. While the *Schützenkompanien* were transported by railway, the automobiles drove to Dachau in a motorized march. In the barracks of the temporarily vacated concentration camp, the men were used to form the *SS-Totenkopf-Division*. The infantrymen arrived in the *SS-Totenkopf-Infanterie-Regiment 3* as a closed *Batallion*, in the same manner as the *13.* and *14./SS-Heimwehr Danzig*, which were taken over as *13.* and *14. Kompanie* in this regiment. The second *Panzerabwehr-Kompanie* formed the basis of the *SS-Totenkopf-Panzerabwehr-Abteilung*.

On October 10, 1939, each member of the *SS-Heimwehr Danzig* in Dachau *"was awarded with the badge of honor of the* SS-Heimwehr Danzig *in memory of his term of service in the* SS-Heimwehr Danzig, *and in memory of the battles for the liberation of Danzig."* With this ended the history of the SS unit after roughly 14 weeks, composed of roughly 1/3 Germans of the Reich, Sudeten-Germans, and citizens of Danzig. The men had completed the tasks put to them, of which the storming of Eichenberg was portrayed as a special achievement.

Set with large propagandistic expenses, the *SS-Heimwehr* fulfilled Himmler's purposes. His *Schutzstaffel* was more than other deployed German units within the same scope, coming into the focus of public attention, and had come a step closer to the desire of social acceptance. Furthermore, he could have taken access of Danzig citizens suitable for the SS before the *Wehrmacht* called on them. For the young Danzig volunteers, however, this meant collective sentencing after the war as members of a criminal organization with all the associated consequences.

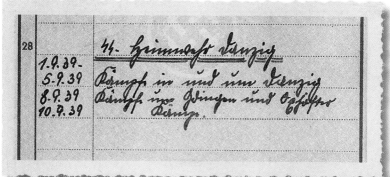

Record in a service record book.

At the end of the combat battle names were determined.

In the first car the *Kommandeur* Goetze.

Behind him the flag bearers.

Return of the *SS-Heimwehr* to Danzig on September 26, 1939

Jubilant reception by the population.

Gauleiter Forster and the wounded *Kommandeur* Goetze.

SS-Hauptsturmführer Baier

Entry into Danzig on September 26, 1939

Entry of the *SS-Heimwehr Danzig* into the vacated Dachau concentration camp, October 1939.

The *Reichsführer-SS* visits the *SS-Heimwehr* in Dachau.

Transfer after Dachau

Signpost in Dachau concentration camp.

Entry of the *Heimwehr* into Dachau.

Assembly in front of one of the watchtowers.

Dachau camp

The *Regimentskommandeur*...

...and several of his honored men.

In Dachau, Goetze became *Kommandeur* of the SS-T.I.R.3.

Formation of *the SS-Totenkopf-Infanterie-Regiment 3* in Dachau

The badge of honor awarded on October 10, 1939

Award certificate for the
badge of honor.

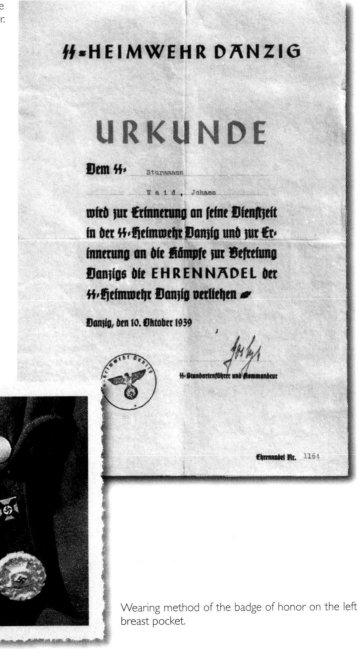

SS-HEIMWEHR DANZIG

URKUNDE

Dem SS- Sturmmann

Waid, Johann

wird zur Erinnerung an seine Dienstzeit
in der SS-Heimwehr Danzig und zur Erinnerung an die Kämpfe zur Befreiung
Danzigs die EHRENNADEL der
SS-Heimwehr Danzig verliehen

Danzig, den 10. Oktober 1939

SS-Standartenführer und Kommandeur

Ehrennadel Nr. 1164

Wearing method of the badge of honor on the left
breast pocket.

The badge of honor awarded on October 10, 1939

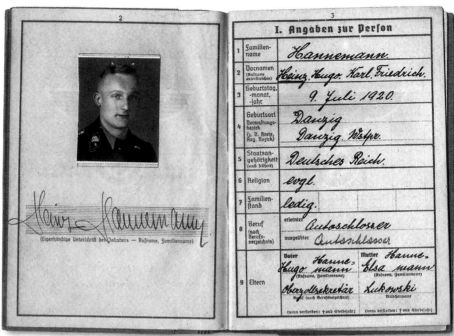

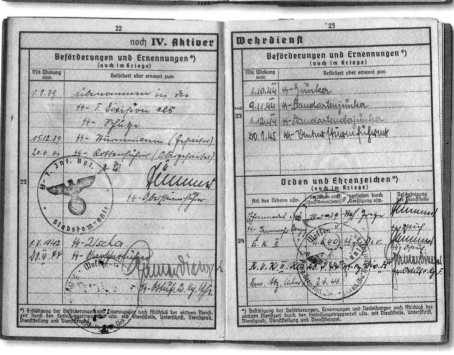

Service record book, with entry of the badge of honor of the *SS-Heimwehr Danzig*

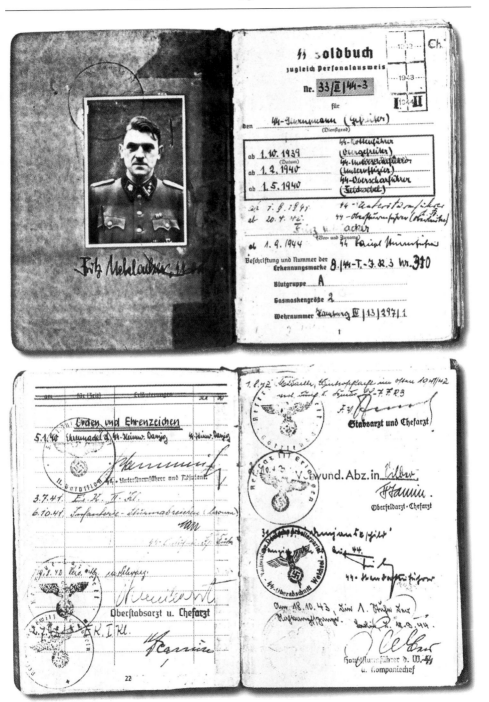

Pay book of the *SS-Hauptsturmführer* Fritz Übelacker

Paul Tergan as *SS-Rottenführer.*

Pay book page with entry of the badge of honor of the *SS-Heimwehr*, and of the K.V.K. 2nd Class with Swords.

Paul Tergan

In August 1939, the Danzig Cross was presented in two classes. The *Kommandeur*, the entire Stab, and the *Kompaniechef* of the *Heimwehr* received the first class, while the *Zugführer* of single *Kompanien* were awarded with the second class.

Entry of the Danzig Cross 1st and 2nd Class in the pay book of *SS-Standartenführer* Goetze.

The *Danzigkreuz*

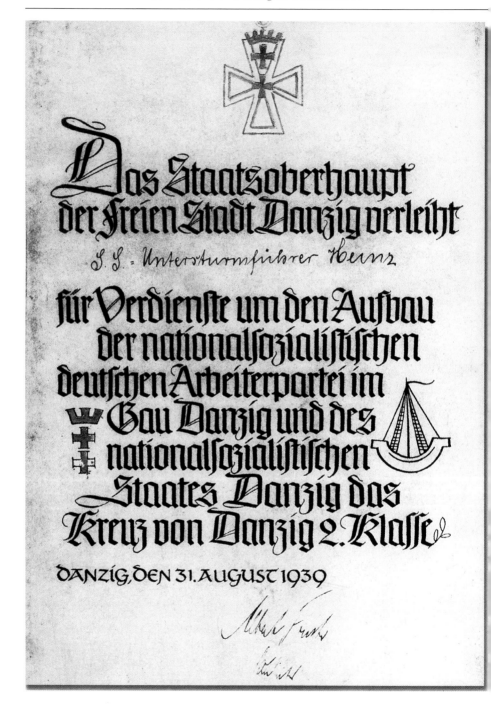

Certificate to the *Danzigkreuz 2. Klasse* for a *SS-Führer* of the *SS-Heimwehr Danzig*

The Organization of German Powers
In and Around Danzig

The deployed German troops in West Prussia were subordinate to the A.O.K. 3, and partially the A.O.K. 4, within the scope of the *Heeresgruppe I* (*Nord*), and were tactically led by the German commander, *General der Flieger* Kaupisch. The *Korps Kaupisch* consisted of:

- the *Grenzschutz-Abschnittskommando* 1 with:
  > 207. *Infanterie-Division* (all units) under its command:
  >> *Stab des Artillerie-Regiment* 609 z. b. V. (mot.)[43]
  >> Heavy *Artillerie-Abteilung* 611 (mot.)[44]
  >> *III./Infanterie-Regiment* 89[45]
  >> *III./Infanterie-Regiment* 48[46]
  >> *II./Artillerie-Regiment* 12
  >> *Grenzwacht-Regiment* 42[47] (Wuth)
  >> *Grenzwacht-Regiment* 32[48] (von Bothmer)
  >>> With subordinate sections of the *SS-Heimwehr Danzig*
- the Brigade Eberhardt (as of September 7, 1939)
  >> with subordinate sections of the *SS-Heimwehr Danzig*

On September 14, 1939, *General der Artillerie* Heitz,[49] as *Militärbefehlshaber* Danzig-Westpreußen, took over the command of the deployed troops of the *Korps Kaupisch*.

---

[43]   The *Artillerie-Regimentsstab* z.b.V. 609 was formed on August 26, 1939, in the *Wehrkreis III*, and assigned as *Heerestruppe* to the *207. Infanterie-Division*.

[44]   The heavy *Artillerie-Abteilung 611* was formed on August 26, 1939, in the *Wehrkreis XIII* with a 10 cm-*Kanonenbattarien* and two heavy *Feldhaubitzen-Battarien*, and came as *Heerestruppe* into the command under the *207. Infanterie-Division*.

[45]   The *Infanterie-Regiment* 89 was established on October 6, 1936, with two *Batallionen* in *Schwerin* for the *12. Infanterie-Division*. The *III. Batallion* was not deployed until the mobilization, and was under the command of the *207. Infanterie-Division*.

[46]   The *Infanterie-Regiment* 48 was established on October 1, 1934, as *Infanterie-Regiment* Döberitz. The renaming followed on October 15, 1935. The Peacetime Station was *Neustrelitz* for the *I.* and *II. Batallion* of the *Regiment* belonging to the *12. Infanterie-Division*. The *III. Btl.* was first formed at mobilization, and was deployed with the *207. Infanterie-Division*.

[47]   The *Grenzwacht-Regiment* 42 was formed on August 26, 1939, in the *Wehrkreis II*, and in Autumn 1939 again disbanded.

[48]   The *Grenzwacht-Regiment* 32 was formed on August 26, 1939, in the *Wehrkreis II*, and in Autumn 1939 again disbanded.

[49]   Walter Heitz was born in Berlin on December 8, 1878. On March 7, 1898, he entered the army as a *Fahnenjunker*, and was appointed to *Leutnant* in the *Feldartillerie-Regiment 36* on August 18, 1899. As *Generalleutnant* (promotion on October 1, 1934) he received the appointment to *Präsident* of the *Reichskriegsgericht* on August 1, 1936. Ranking as a *General* of the *Artillerie* (April 1, 1937), Heitz was appointed *Militärbefehlshaber* Danzig-Westpreußen. Afterwards, as of October 25, 1939, he led the *VIII. Armee-Korps*, and one day after the appointment to *Generaloberst*, on January 31, 1939, he came into Soviet war captivity in Stalingrad, in which he died in Moscow in 1944. He was honored with the German Cross in gold, and the *Knight's Cross mit Eichenlaub*.

The Danzig *Vorposten* wrote about this on September 26, 1939:

"Yesterday afternoon at 1600 hours, in the Generalkommando's *home, the celebratory act of the presentation of his home to* General der Artillerie *Heitz through* Gauleiter *Albert Forster took place. The* General *was received by the* Gauleiter *in the hall of the home, and was greeted with a short speech....*
The Militärbefehlshaber *Danzig-Westpreußen,* General der Artillerie *Heitz, thanked the* Gauleiter *with touching words, and explained among others:*
    'I am aware of the historical importance of this moment. The fact that I take over this house through your introduction is symbolic for the event that is currently taking place. We, who exchange a genuine handshake at this place, embody both pillars of the Greater German Reich. You, as the first political representative of the National Socialist movement in Danzig, and I as a representative of the Wehrmacht, *the other pillar. It is our duty to together master the tasks that we must accomplish!'*
After this dignified act, the Militärbefehlshaber *proceeded back to his office, which is still found in the building of the earlier Polish Gymnasium."*

Staffing and Forces Postal Service Numbers

The organization of the *SS-Heimwehr Danzig* that, in addition to four *Schützen-Kompanien*, also included a *Kraftfahr-* and *Infanterie-Geschütz*, as well as two *Panzerabwehr-Kompanien*[50]. It is also interesting that altogether nine leaders commanded *Kompanien*, which had nearly exclusively four, instead of two to three *Züge*:[51]

Kommandeur	*SS-Obersturmbannführer* Goetze	F.P.Nr. 09723
Adjutant	*SS-Obersturmführer* Westermann	
Stab	*SS-Hauptsturmführer* Sparmann	F.P.Nr. 24611
O.O.	*SS-Untersturmführer* Valtin	
1. Verwaltungsführer	*SS-Obersturmführer* Hagen	
2. Verwaltungsführer	*SS-Untersturmführer* Buschardt	
Nachrichtenzugführer	*SS-Untersturmführer* Stieglitz	
Meldezugführer	*SS-Untersturmführer* Hartrampft	
Pionierzugführer	*SS-Untersturmführer* Knaak	
Kraftfahrkompanie	*SS-Obersturmführer* Schneider	
I. Zug	*SS-Untersturmführer* Heins	
II. Zug	*SS-Untersturmführer* Dümmer	
III. Zug	*SS-Untersturmführer* Schultz	
1. Schüten-Kompanie	*SS-HauptsturmfÜhrer* Their	F.P.Nr. 24293
I. Zug	*SS-Untersturmführer* Peiper	
II. Zug	*SS-Untersturmführer* Gnabs	
III. Zug	*SS-Untersturmführer* Radünz	
IV. Zug	*SS-Untersturmführer* Weiter	
2. Schützen-Kompanie	*SS-Obersturmführer* Bredemeier	F.P.Nr. 31292
I. Zug	*SS-Obersturmführer* Prechtl	
II. Zug	*SS-Untersturmführer* Kersten	
III. Zug	*SS-Oberscharführer* Lindner	
IV. Zug		
3. Schützen-Kompanie	*SS-Hauptsturmführer* Urbanitz[52]	F.P.Nr. 31700
I. Zug	*SS-Obersturmführer* Prechtl	

---

[50]   The availability of two *Panzerabwehr-Kompanien* displays the originally planned, defensive area of responsibility of the *SS-Heimwehr Danzig*.

[51]   The strength approximately corresponded to that of a later *SS-Sturmbrigade* (newer type).

[52]   Urbanitz was not popular. A former member of the *Waffen-SS* remembers: "*SS-Hauptsturmführer* Urbanitz was head of the *Kanonenbatterie* by us. He was initially *Kompaniechef* with the *SS-Heimwehr Danzig* and the *SS-Totenkopf-Division* and around August 1941 he came to the *LAH*. He also did not have a good reputation with us. When in September/October 1941 a comrade of ours was fatally wounded, he said while dying: Smack the Urbanitz in the puss! Also, when he took over the heavy *Korps-Artillerie-Abteilung* in May 1944 he could not last long and had to give up the detachment. I think, he then came to Götz von Berlichingen. Whoever was pushed around to so many units, he was actually unqualified as a leader and thus unpopular. Not every leader was a model!"

II. Zug	*SS-Untersturmführer* Bahrend	
III. Zug	*SS-Untersturmführer* Frommhagen	
IV. Zug	*SS-Oberscharführer* Oberschmitt	
4. Schützen-Kompanie	*SS-Obersturmführer* Braun	F.P.Nr. 32304
I. Zug	*SS-Untersturmführer* Hilgenstock	
II. Zug	*SS-Untersturmführer* Zorn	
III. Zug	*SS-Untersturmführer* Wagner	
IV. Zug	*SS-Untersturmführer* Mützelfeld	
MG-Kompanie	*SS-Hauptsturmführer* Baier	F.P.Nr. 33094
(I.G.) Kompanie	*SS-Hauptsturmführer* Schulz	F.P.Nr. 33475
I. Zug	*SS-Hauptsturmführer* Kühn	
II. Zug	*SS-Untersturmführer* Hiermeyer	
III. Zug	*SS-Obersturmführer* Walter	
1. (Pak.) Kompanie	*SS-Hauptsturmführer* Steiner[53]	F.P.Nr. 33832
2. (Pak.) Kompanie	*SS-Obersturmführer* Leiner	F.P.Nr. 34799
I. Zug	*SS-Untersturmführer* Vogel	
II. Zug	*SS-Untersturmführer* Zipp	

---

53   Steiner was *Zugführer* in the *7./SS-Totenkopf-Standarte 1 Oberbayern* in 1938.

The Fallen Soldiers of the *SS-Heimwehr Danzig*

SS-Unterscharführer	Albert, Georg	Dirschau
SS-Anwärter	Bach, Günter	Dirschau
SS-Mann	Behrendt, Günter	Oxhöfter Kämpe
SS-Anwärter	Bieland, Alfons	Oxhöfter Kämpe
SS-Mann	Blankenberg	Dirschau
SS-Mann	Böbel	Oxhöfter Kämpe
SS-Rottenführer	Böhm, Paul	Dirschau
SS-Mann	Fauth, Hans-Werner	Dirschau
SS-Mann	Fensk, Manfred	Dirschau
SS-Rottenführer	Fleßner, Meinhard	Dirschau
SS-Anwärter	Flohr, Walter	Dirschau
SS-Sturmmann	Fuchs	Dirschau
SS-Mann	Goebel, Günter	
SS-Anwärter	Haubaum, Eduard	Oxhöfter Kämpe
SS-Mann	Heise, Gerhard	Oxhöfter Kämpe
SS-Sturmmann	Hipler, Paul	Dirschau
SS-Anwärter	Irmler, Günter	
SS-Anwärter	Kindl, Werner	Oxhöfter Kämpe
SS-Anwärter	Köster, Bernhard	Rheda
SS-Mann	Körnig, Walter	Dirschau
	Lehmann, Hermann	
SS-Anwärter	Marschall, Hans	Dirschau
SS-Mann	Obeth, Rudolf	Dirschau
SS-Obersturmführer	Oppel, Oppel	Oxhöfter Kämpe
SS-Rottenführer	Patzak, Erwin	Oxhöfter Kämpe
SS-Unterscharführer	Patzlaff, Walter	Dirschau
SS-Schütze	Prinz, Heinz	Dirschau
SS-Oberscharführer	Schahd	Dirschau
SS-Anwärter	Schankin, Paul	Dirschau
SS-Anwärter	Schimikowski, Franz	
SS-Oberscharführer	Schlag, Herbert	Dirschau
SS-Schütze	Schuma, Alexander	Dirschau
SS-Sturmmann	Schumacher	Dirschau
SS-Scharführer	Stark, Alois	Dirschau
SS-Scharführer	Strathausen	Oxhöfter Kämpe
SS-Rottenführer	Teynor, Hans	Polish Post Office
SS-Schütze	Uhlig, Siegfried	Oxhöfter Kämpe
SS-Untersturmführer	Weiter, Alois	Dirschau
SS-Obersturmführer	Westermann	Oxhöfter Kämpe

Gewehrführer from 1. Zug sMG.

Cemetery of honor for the fallen citizens of Danzig.

The Danzig military cemetery in *Silberhammer*

Im begeisterten Glauben an den Sieg unseres Führers fiel am 24. April 1942 in Sowjetrußland an der Spitze seiner Kompanie mein lieber Mann, der gute Vater meines kleinen Jungen, unser lieber, einziger Sohn, Bruder, Schwiegersohn, Schwager u. Onkel

Hanns Radünz

ℋ-Obersturmführer in der Waffen-ℋ

Inh. d. EK. I u. II, d. Inf.-Sturmabzeichens, des Danziger Kreuzes II. Kl., der Ehrennadel d. ℋ-Heimwehr Danzig, des Verwundetenabzeichens, des Goldenen HJ.-Ehrenzeichens und anderer Auszeichnungen im 26. Lebensjahr.

Gerta Radünz, geb. Michel, und Sohn Ekkehard; Willy Radünz und Frau Hedwig, geb. Treder; Feldwebel u. Offz.-Anw. Paul Gillach u. Frau Eva, geb. Radünz; Hauptmann Heinz Reschke, zZ. im Felde, und Frau Käthe, geb. Radünz; Louis Michel und Frau Anna, geb. Seepe; Hugo Westebbe u. Frau Anni, geb. Michel.

Unna, Kolberg, Neustettin und Großenhain, den 12. Mai 1942

Am 22. September fiel im Osten auf dem Felde der Ehre unser lieber, guter Junge, unser immer hilfsbereiter, inniggeliebter, ältester Bruder,

stud. arch.

Erhard Liebert

ℋ-Standarten-Oberjunker und Zugführer in einer MG-Kompanie

ausgezeichnet mit den EK II. Kl., dem Danziger Kreuz II. Kl und der Ehrennadel der ℋ-Heimwehr im blühenden Alter von 21 Jahren, nach glücklich überstandenen Kämpfen in Polen und Frankreich.

In opferbereitem Einsatz gab er getreu dem Fahneneid sein junges Leben für Deutschlands Größe und wurde fern der befreiten Heimat auf einem Heldenfriedhof in fremder Erde zur letzten Ruhe gebettet.

In tiefer Trauer
Im Namen der Hinterbliebenen

Adalbert Liebert und Frau Elsa geb. Dünnbier.

Danzig, den 10 Oktober 1941,
Hundegasse 103.

Den Soldatentod für Führer und Volk starb am 25. Mai 1940 bei den Kämpfen am La-Bassée-Kanal der

ℋ-Mann

Horst Bark

Wir werden ihm stets ein ehrendes Andenken bewahren.

Launer
ℋ-Hauptsturmführer u. Komp.-Chef in der Waffen-ℋ

Den Heldentod für Führer und Großdeutschland starb am 27. Mai 1940 bei Le Paradis der

ℋ-Sturmmann

Artur Krause

Er war uns ein lieber Kamerad. Wir werden ihn nie vergessen.

Launer
ℋ-Hauptsturmführer u. Komp.-Chef in der Waffen-ℋ

Im begeisterten, freiwilligen Einsatz für Führer und Vaterland, in treuer, heldenhafter Pflichterfüllung, getreu seinem Fahneneide, fiel am 24. Oktober 1941 im Kampfe gegen den Bolschewismus in einem Stoßtrupp unser vielgeliebter Sohn, Bruder, Schwager und Onkel

Rudolf Kling

ℋ - Unter-Scharführer, Träger des E. K. II., des Verwundetenabzeichens, der silbernen Ehrennadel der ℋ - Heimwehr Danzig,

im 22. Lebensjahre.

Bransdorf, im November 1941.

In tiefster Trauer:

Hildegard, Friedrich, Maria Kling, Anna Anders   Gerhard Anders
als Geschwister   als Schwager

Renate Kling
als Nichte

und sämtliche Verwandten

Druck: Jägerndorfer Zeitung

In treuer Pflichterfüllung fiel am 27. Mai 1940 im Gefecht bei Le Paradies für Führer und Vaterland der

ℋ-Mann

Hans Schulz

Wir werden diesen tapferen Kameraden nie vergessen.

Launer
ℋ-Hauptsturmführer u. Komp.-Chef in der Waffen-ℋ

Fallen former members of the *SS-Heimwehr Danzig*

Epilogue

"Despite the hardest experiences in war captivity and internment, as well as conviction as members of a criminal organization, the largest portion of former soldiers of the Waffen-SS *have proven through willingness to work and discipline that they are ready to accept and support a democratic form of government.*

Success and disappointments shift in the postwar years. Many hopes are not fulfilled, and our wishes that justice befalls us cannot be entirely actualized.

Thus, in the postwar period comradeship developed in which former members of the Waffen-SS *found each other again, and helped each other out when necessary.*

Comrade, where are you?, I also thought as a former Danzig volunteer, and founded a tracing service. I wanted to know how many of the old comrades were still alive. The first tracing service took place on June 7-8, 1975, in Coburg. At this meeting, the decision was made to establish a troop comradeship, *which was realized one year later.*

Wolfram Schneider was the first speaker, and I was appointed as managing director. Many meetings followed, and the solidarity grew again. The meetings gave much to all parties involved. It showed that loyalty is not an empty word."

Leo Wilm
1. Geschäftsführer der Truppenkameradschaft

Ranks *SS/Wehrmacht*

SS-Anwärter	1st Year of Service[54]	*Schütze*
SS-Mann	2nd Year of Service	*Oberschütze*
SS-Sturmmann	3rd Year of Service	*Gefreiter*
SS-Rottenführer	4th Year of Service	*Obergefreiter*
SS-Unterscharführer	Unteroffizier	
SS-Scharführer	*Unterfeldwebel*	
SS-Oberscharführer	*Feldwebel*	
SS-Hauptscharführer	*Oberfeldwebel*	
SS-Untersturmführer	*Leutnant*	
SS-Obersturmführer	*Oberleutnant*	
SS-Hauptsturmführer	*Hauptmann*	
SS-Sturmbannführer	*Major*	
SS-Obersturmbannführer	*Oberstleutnant*	
SS-Standartenführer	*Oberst*	
SS-Oberführer	no comparable rank	
SS-Brigadeführer	*Generalmajor*	
SS-Gruppenführer	*Generalleutnant*	
SS-Obergruppenführer	*General*	
SS-Oberstgruppenführer	*Generaloberst*	

---

[54] The ranks should strictly conform to term of service according to the *Geheime Kommandosache Nr. 10470/34* of the *Allgemeines Heeresamt* from November 13, 1934. This was modified over the course of time, however, was valid with restrictions still in 1939 with the *SS-Heimwehr Danzig*.

Bibliography

Bachmann, Hans: *Hela in: Wehrwissenschaftliche* Rundschau 1970

Keilig, Wolf: *Das Deutsche Heer 1939 – 1945*, Bad Nauheim 1957

Klietmann Dr., Kurt: *Die Waffen-SS*, Osnabrück 1980

Lewald, Hans: *Danzig – so wie es war*, Düsseldorf 1974

Meyer Dr., Hans Bernhard (Hrsg.): *Danzig in 144 Bildern*, Leer 1956

Michaelis, Rolf: Die Geschichte der *SS-Heimwehr Danzig*, Rodgau 1990

Müller, G., Guthmann, F.: *Die Geschichte der 207. und 281. Infanterie-Division*, Dortmund 1958

Schindler, Herbert: *Mosty und Dirschau 1939*, Freiburg 1971

Stjerfeld, Bertil, Böhme, Klaus-Richard: *Westerplatte 1939*, Freiburg 1979

Tessin, Georg: *Verbände und Truppen der deutschen Wehrmacht und Waffen-SS im 2. Weltkrieg*, Osnabrück 1980 ff.

Vormann von, Nikolaus: *Der Feldzug 1939 in Polen*, Weissenburg 1958

Ohne: *Beiträge zur Geschichte der 60. Infanterie-Division (mot.)*, o.O., 1979

Sought:
Photographs, Award Certificates,
Pay Books, and Service Record Books
As well as reports based on experiences
Of former participants in the war

Michaelis-Verlag
Postfach 950 164
12 461 Berlin

The SS-Panzer-Artillery Regiment 1 Leibstandarte Adolf Hitler (LAH) in World War II

Thomas Fischer

This book is the first volume about Artillery Regiment 1 of the 1st Waffen-SS Division Leibstandarte Adolf Hitler (LAH). The artillery batteries of the LAH during the whole of World War II faced some of the hardest combat, and probably no other artillery unit was used as often at critical spots on all fronts. While it had only three batteries of light field howitzers during the French campaign, when the full artillery regiment was set up in August 1940, it later received heavier guns and 88mm flak. In April 1941, at Lake Kastoria in Macedonia during a tremendous artillery battle, the full regiment fired as a unit for the first time. During the battles on the Russian Front the regiment's artillery equipment was constantly upgraded. One of the artillery batteries was equipped from 1943 with Wespe and Hummel self-propelled guns and later with Nebelwerfer rocket launchers that gave the regiment its tremendous firepower. Especially during the difficult defensive battles in the winter of 1943-1944 in the Ukraine, every artillery piece - whether a heavy field howitzer, or 15cm rocket launcher - was often used at such close range that it was fired with barrels in a horizontal position. The battery was later attached to the reconnaissance unit in the vanguard of the LAH and experienced the hardest battles while using "Panzermeyer tactics" that required rapid marches and lightning fast deployment into firing positions. Nearly 300 photos, most never before published, document the bitter battles of the LAH artillery regiment.

8 1/2" x 11"   over 290 b/w photos   208 pp   hard cover

ISBN: 0764319825 $59.95

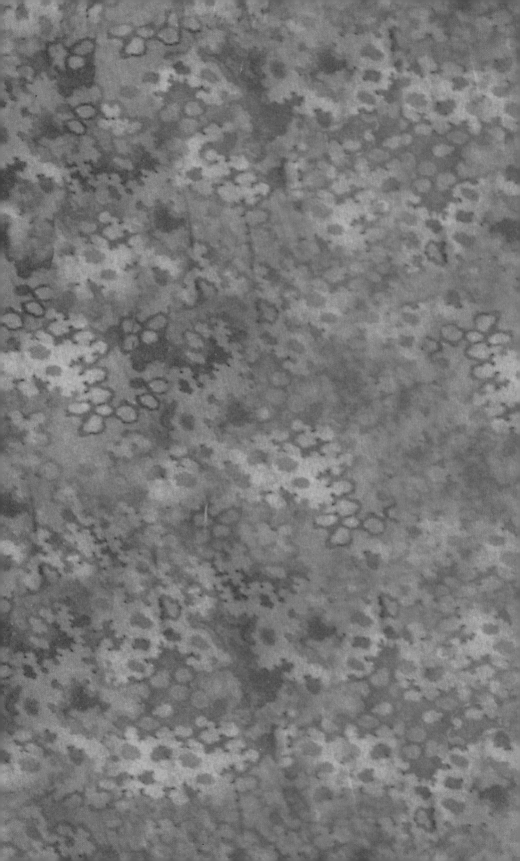